MANAGERS
THE DAY AFTER TOMORROW

This book was originally published as *Managers the day after tomorrow*, LannooCampus Publishers & Van Duuren Management (2018).

D/2018/45/348 – ISBN 978 94 014 5423 0 – NUR 801

Cover and interior design: Peer De Maeyer
Illustrations: Steve Reynders
Author portrait: Sarah Oyserman
Translation: Ian Connerty

LannooCampus Publishers is a subsidiary of Lannoo Publishers, the book and multimedia division of Lannoo Publishers nv.

LannooCampus Publishers
Erasme Ruelensvest 179 box 101
3001 Leuven
Belgium
www.lannoocampus.be

RIK VERA

MANAGERS
THE DAY AFTER TOMORROW

Connect to many
Engage individuals

LANNOO
CAMPUS

PREFACE

I am writing this foreword on 21 March 2018. I am in Miami. Outside, it is summer.

I have begun a new version about thirty times so far. Each time I start by making a list of the people I shouldn't forget to mention. But the list just keeps on growing. Unfortunately, that doesn't mean the likelihood of forgetting someone gets smaller. Quite the reverse. Worse still, the length of the list is inversely proportional to the possibility that the person I forget will hold it against me.

Where I am, who I am and the fact that my daily activities coincide almost exactly with that 'who I am' is not something I can take all the credit for. I am a dreamer. Full stop

This book is a kind of summary, a compilation of everything that has happened before. It is the product of all the people I know and all the things that have happened in my life so far. Not my choices. I have never been good at making choices. I am water, and the people around me have guided the flow. Some more profoundly than others. I make no distinction between positive and negative. Everyone and everything has played a role.

I would like to thank you all. For the warmth. For the support. For the love. Dreamers need that.

We have a crushing responsibility. We need to shape the world for the sake of our children and grandchildren. All of us. Including the managers of today and tomorrow. I hope they will do so with The Day After Tomorrow in mind. I hope that they can help their companies adapt to the new world in which my grandchildren will grow up.

With this in mind, I dedicate this book to Line and Nout, my grandchildren.

*'History doesn't repeat itself,
but it often rhymes.'*

MARK TWAIN

PROLOGUE

BE ONE
OR BE ZERO

January 2018. The dark sky of a short winter's day, full of scudding clouds, with a splash of blue here and there. Orange too. And red. Perfectly normal for this time of year. Several chapters of this book are already on my hard drive. A book in the making. Some of these collections of words and ideas look more like a proper chapter than others. Some still need polishing up. Quite a lot of polishing up. Others are more or less ready, at least in terms of content. Or that is what I thought when I wrote them a couple of months ago. However, now that I am reading them again, screen by screen, I realize that I need to revise and rebuild much of the text. Time corrodes both content and structure. Today, faster than ever before.

I try to think of new building blocks and how I can fit them together. I check to see where I don't have enough material and where I need to scrap things. Too much or too little. Up to date or out of date. Believe me, writing a book intended to serve as a manual for the managers of The Day After Tomorrow is an exercise in mental agility like no other!

What is the best strategy for the digital world? How can you deal with unpredictability? How is it possible, both as an entrepreneur and as an enterprise, to keep in sync with the outside world, the world of technology <u>and</u> the world of the consumer? Where do you focus your attention? Which of the countless possibilities do you explore? How can you redesign your company to make it sustainably relevant? Which technological wave do you need to surf? What do you have to build up and what do you have to tear down?

The questions I want to answer are already in my head... plenty of them. However, it is a feature of our rapidly changing world that there is no longer a single answer to any of these questions. The moment you give one, you already need to think about how you can best modify it. It is impossible to work with a prefab design when developing a strategy for the digital world. You need to build systematically, block by block, adjusting and amending as you go, so that you can keep up with the changing fashions and opportunities of the day.

In this book I lay bare the vectors that govern our changing world. I also seek to explode the myths behind many of the current hypes. I will talk about mirrors, the underworld, and the overturning of the world as we know it. About *slow architecture,* about building cathedrals, about sharks and red oceans. I draw my inspiration from Gaudi, from Escher, from *Stranger Things* and from Mars.

It does not suffice to add a sprinkle of digital dust to your company. To develop an effective strategy for the digital world, you need to understand how the world is evolving beyond the limits of your classical range of vision. You need to know which forces and underground currents are influencing each other.

The digital world is turning – and will continue to turn – many of our existing realities and markets upside down. The new business models that are so successful today at disrupting the old models are, in fact, nothing more than those old models turned upside down. Even today, I meet managers and entrepreneurs who are still locked in their familiar and understandable world above the surface, without having the faintest idea of what is happening in the parallel world beneath that surface, where new subcultures are emerging and mutating at an astonishing speed.

It is not the internet that has changed the world. The world has been changed by companies who have had the courage and the wisdom to turn their thinking upside down, who have developed with, through and on the internet, but not because of it. The internet is a tool, not a cause. These companies use technology to get around the limitations of conventional business models and to combine the advantages of mass production with hyper-connectivity and hyper-personalization. Such companies do little more than mirror existing models, but the reflection this mirror casts is governed by digital laws. Typically, this kind of disrupter company remains under the radar of the established order for a long time, until they suddenly break the surface – and by then, it's too late to do much about it. Consumers, as we all know, change with the wind. As soon as they have sampled the benefits and the ease of the new mirror model, they will no longer settle for less. And we are all consumers, we all increasingly live in this crazy, new, upside-down world. In fact, we have become that world.

Companies are still far too inclined to think in terms of the product. They believe it is only possible to break open a market with radically innovative products or new technologies. That is not so. It is not about new products or new technologies. It is about changing consumer behaviour. Being one with the customer or being zero. Maximizing value or having no value what-soever: that is the choice facing organizations today. Companies are at a turning point, whether they like it or not. The world has been turned upside down. The top is now at the bottom, and the bottom at the top. Technology has given the customer power. The connected customer weighs his options and decides. It is he (or she, of course) who makes your marketing.

It is still possible to build new, large and successful organizations by tapping into today's saturated markets, even with what may seem like existing business models, but only if those models make optimal use of the new laws of the new world and are able to persuade consumers to make the change with you. That is the core of my book: how you, as a manager, can understand these new laws and how you can take your first steps towards this brave new world.

For some people, reading a book is a chore. For the speed-readers among you, who kick on key words and quotes, here is some advice: always look at things from the perspective of the customer. We are all people, and people can understand each other. Technology is only a threat for those who are not willing to explore its possibilities. The better you understand your customer and the closer you are able to stand by him, the easier it will be to find the right technological wave to surf, so that you will always be fully on board, living in the moment with your customer – and not after it.

Rik Vera

CONTENT

5   THE NEW BUSINESS MODEL   142

*'What's not going to change
in the next ten years?'*
JEFF BEZOS, CEO AMAZON

FAST FORWARD SLOW ARCHITECTURE

When I was looking for an image to explain to managers how they can develop a strategy for the digital world, I was suddenly struck by the idea of a great Gothic cathedral. The kind of cathedral you can see in Antwerp, Cologne, Reims, Chartres or York. These cathedrals were built to the greater glory of God, who lived, of course, in heaven. This meant they had to be as tall as possible, reaching as near to heaven as they could. Successive layers of arches and high stained glass windows served to strengthen this sense of the vertical.

The building of these Houses of God spanned a number of generations, sometimes even centuries. The original design evolved as time passed and fashions changed, and was strongly influenced by the funds available, the wishes of the people commissioning the work and new technical insights. In most of these cathedrals, like the Cathedral of Our Lady in Antwerp, built between 1352 and 1521, you can usually see a series of different architectural styles, built one on top of the other, both inside and out. The same applies to the materials used. In Antwerp, no fewer than thirty different types of sandstone were used in the cathedral's construction. Similarly, the best available building techniques of the moment were employed. These kept pace with the progress of the church and were sometimes developed specifically, when a seemingly impossible technical problem was encountered. However, finding a solution was only possible by moving beyond 'traditional' patterns of thinking. One insight led to another.

Interesting detail about the Cathedral of Our Lady in Antwerp: unlike most others in northern Europe, it was not built on the remains of an earlier Romanesque church. It was actually built *around* a Romanesque church, which was only demolished in 1487, when the cathedral was already half completed. In other words, for 125 years the people of Antwerp worshipped their God in a church that was surrounded by a construction site! What is more, a construction site where there was constant activity: an adjustment here, a different function there and new techniques almost everywhere. Renovation sometimes even had to be carried out on the parts of the structure that had already been completed.

None of these cathedrals were built according to an ideal plan. The plan simply followed customer demand. Once again, Antwerp is typical. Its layout was altered several times. Economic growth in the course of the two centuries of its construction made the local guilds and craftsmen wealthy, so that they each wanted their own chapel or altar. As a result, the church had to be made longer and wider than originally planned.[2]

Ideally, a Gothic cathedral should have seven towers: two at the front of the nave, four to mark the transept and one to rise above the crossing. Once again, none of Europe's Gothic cathedrals have this configuration. In other words, none of them were completed the way originally envisaged. The image we see today, no matter how symbolic the cathedral in question might be for its city and no matter how deeply its appearance is rooted in our imagination, is therefore an incomplete image of an unfinished building. You can regard the Gothic cathedrals as a 'work in progress', an expression in stone and glass of the evolving economic and political history of a city or region, up to the point where that evolution came to an end, either because the money ran out or because consumers now wanted something different in other markets.

'THE BUILDING OF A COMPANY IS LIKE THE SLOW BUILDING OF A CATHEDRAL – ONLY FASTER.'

Why am I telling you this story of the cathedrals? The answer is simple: to make clear that there is a parallel with how a company can and should be built in our changing world. To begin with, you need a ground plan, an objective and some foundations. Once you have these, you can set to work, sometimes on top of or around an existing business model, sometimes alongside it, but always with the same progressive insight at the heart of all you do. From the very first moment, you need to be aware that the plan, the technology, the techniques and the tools will all change dramatically as your project – whatever it might be – progresses in the months and years ahead.

Building a cathedral is a lengthy process. Companies in the modern world need to move much faster and must be able to recognize (and respond to) the rapidly changing demands of fickle consumers. If you fail to mir-

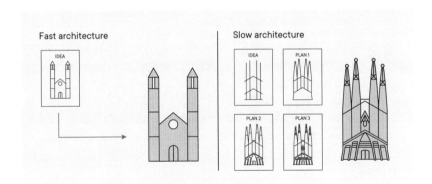

Fast architecture   Slow architecture

Fast Architecture versus Slow Architecture

ror what your customers want, you will be lost. The need for progressive insight remains a constant.

Smart entrepreneurs make use of what I call *fast forward slow architecture*. For me, *slow architecture* is the architecture of progressive insight. First, there is the dream. Next, the rough plans and budgeting. Only then can you implement your project, using lots and lots of progressive insight, applied with maximum flexibility. The building of a company is like the slow building of a cathedral – only faster.

In Barcelona you can see a real-life example of *slow architecture*. Since 1882, work has been taking place on the construction of the *Basílica i Temple Expiatori de la Sagrada Família,* the vision of a brilliant but eccentric genius, Antoni Gaudí. It is a church of reconciliation, and, according to the laws of the Catholic Church, such churches must be financed entirely by the donations of the faithful. This makes the Sagrada Família perhaps the most famous unknown crowdfunding project avant la lettre in history! The official date for its completion is to be somewhere in 2026, but it might just as easily be later. 2026 would be appropriate, because it is a significant date on the Gaudí time line. On 7 June 1926, the absent-minded Gaudí accidentally walked under the wheels of Tram No. 30 at the corner of Gran Via and *carrer* Bailén.[1] He died three days later.

Gaudí is often called an architect, but that is not really what he was. An architect draws a detailed plan, has everything calculated down to the finest detail by engineers, and makes a specification in which the materials and techniques to be employed are listed exhaustively. Gaudí did none of that. He was a man of philosophical concepts, a man with images in his head, which he visualized for others in a few brief sketches and simple models, but always infused with his keen sense of progressive insight. For Gaudí, there was no difference between the structure of a building and its decoration.[4] Everything was a single organic entity. The Sagrada was his vision of what a basilica should be, developed on the earlier foundations of his predecessor Francisco de Paula del Villar – who was a more traditional architect – and constructed with little thought for margins of safety, relying instead on a kind of improvised experimentalism. It was not until 1906 that a definitive plan was finally agreed upon – 24 years after the first stone had been laid.

Gaudí worked on the Sagrada for 43 years. From 1914 onwards, he was active there almost non-stop.[5] In his final years, he even lived on site, so that he would lose as little time as possible. All the work that has been carried out on the church since his death in 1926 is based on an interpretation of Gaudí's general design, detail plans and plaster models. If the pace of this work has speeded up in recent years, this is not only due to an increase in the number of donations, but also to the use of simulation software from the aviation industry, which allows the engineers to make accurate calculations for Gaudí's organic twisted columns and his hyperboloid and hyperbolic paraboloid roof vaults.[6]

Gaudí followed formal architectural training at the Escola Technica d'Arquitectura, but found it a waste of time. According to him, it lacked all creativity. He thought he was light years ahead of the limited insights of his teachers and he had no qualms about telling them so. When Gaudí graduated in 1878, the school director Elie Rogent said: *'He aprobado a un loco o a un genio'* (I have just given a diploma to someone who is either a fool or a genius).[7]

When I first visited Barcelona in the 1980s, you could still wander around the building site, more or less undisturbed. However, then the tourists started to arrive, in ever greater numbers, especially since the Olympic Games in 1992. Today, people from all over the world come to Barcelona – in droves. Some 4.5 million tourists now visit Sagrada Família each year, twice as many as a decade ago.

In the museum I was able admire the master's dark, almost abstract drawings, the contours of what Sagrada Família must one day become. The museum is still there, but nowadays you need to reserve your ticket and a time slot online. I can still remember the high, vaulted spaces and, above all, Gaudí's hanging chain models, which he made in mirror image (standing over mirrors to do it), using pieces of cord and chain, from which he hung little bags filled with lead pellets.[8] In essence, the Sagrada was designed upside down and then hung from the ceiling.

Gaudi devoted ten years of his life to perfecting his 'hanging chain' method of design, which would serve as an upside down version of the arched forms he sought. You first trace the outline of the ground plan, the basic idea of the building you have in your head, on a wooden board. Next, you fix this wooden board to the roof, so that you can start hanging chains with small weights attached to the points where the columns and arches must come. This creates a hanging, three-dimensional model of the idealized form for those columns and arches. All you then need to do is measure everything, photograph the model from various angles, turn the resulting images upside down, and then you can get started with the actual construction. Sounds simple? Perhaps – but it is not. It is science and mathematics at the highest level. Gaudi's discovery still influences scientists today, so much so that in 2004 MIT offered a workshop based on his methods![9]

So when you stroll through the Sagrada Familia, admiring the forest of columns and pausing to glance up at the undulations of the vaults, remember that you are actually looking down into the depths rather than up into the heights, and that you are walking upside down in an upside down world. Once you come to accept this notion, a whole new universe will open up for you.

When I tried to explain to a group of managers a few weeks ago that building a strategy for the digital world is similar to the accelerated slow building of a cathedral, with *fast forward slow architecture,* I used this image of the Sagrada basilica as a metaphor for the challenges they face: building with a vision, with a basis inherited from elsewhere, with an initial but incom-

Reverse architecture

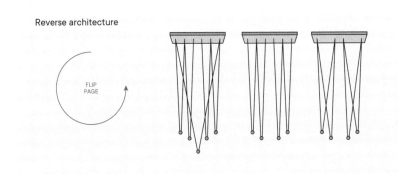

FLIP
PAGE

'TURN YOUR BUSINESS MODEL UPSIDE DOWN. OR TURN IT BACK TO FRONT. LOOK AT WHAT IS – AND THEN DESIGN ITS MIRROR IMAGE.'

plete plan and with a huge amount of progressive insight. The originality of Gaudí – his 'out-of-the-boxness', if you like – was his revolutionary new method of design. You can compare him with Elon Musk and his remarkable dreams. Or with Steve Jobs and the way he gave instructions to his people: just a brief sketch of an almost unachievable goal, to serve as an image that people can then work towards.

I want to help you as a reader to gain access to a changing world, to a world where an inverted form of logic applies that is different to the world you know and are familiar with, a world that is a mirror image of today's tried and trusted models and which uses existing elements in radically different ways.

As a manager in the Age of the New Normal, it is smart to learn to think like Gaudí. Turn your business model upside down. Or turn it back to front. Look at what is – and then design its mirror image. Reverse traditional rolls. If a chain currently runs from left to right, let it run from right to left – or vice versa. Or turn it upside down. Or around. But always with the customer in a central position. Think about existing technology and which bits of it are necessary to successfully implement your mirror-image plan. It is that inverted image, the image behind the mirror, that I want you to grasp from this book.

'Gonna put an old school drive-in, roller skates & rock restaurant at one of the new Tesla Supercharger locations in LA.'

ELON MUSK

1

DISRUPTION IS NORMAL

Faster than you think

James (Jamie for his friends) Dimon is board chairman and CEO of J.P. Morgan Chase, the largest of the big American banks. Jamie is also a man who likes to speak his mind plainly. Even bluntly. So I notice each time I read an article from or with him in the press, online and elsewhere. He also regularly writes long letters to his shareholders. In one of these letters, he admits that he sometimes lays awake at night, worrying. Not about the last bank crisis, or the fierce competition from other banks, or even about all the many evils in the world. No, Jamie loses his good night's sleep because he is worried about the 'hoodies' who run the start-ups in Silicon Valley, the men and women with their sweat-shirts, pony-tails and flip flops, and – more importantly – their bitcoins and alternative fintech. '*When I go to Silicon Valley … they all want to eat our lunch,*' complained Dimon. '*Silicon Valley is coming and if banks don't up their game, then tech companies will take over the industry's business.*'

There are a couple of surprising things here: not only that Dimon made his complaint in public, but also that he was soon forced to eat his own words. Or at least moderate his tone. In September 2017, Dimon compared bitcoin with '*a fraud*'.[10] Just a few months later, at the start of 2018, he was much more restrained in his claims and added that '*the blockchain is real.*'[11] Progressive insight works. If the CEO of America's largest financial institution loses his beauty sleep because of start-ups who want to hijack his bank's business model only to embrace it a short while later, clearly something is awry. Today, J.P. Morgan invests hundreds of millions of dollars in new technology projects worldwide, much of it in fintech and in partnerships with promising fintech companies. In addition, J.P. Morgan is also working in-house to develop its own blockchain programme, the Interbank Information Network, with the aim of simplifying the transaction chain for international payments, thereby making the payment process quicker and cheaper than ever before.[12]

Jamie Dimon has admitted that he made three crucial underestimations in recent times. His first underestimation relates to the impact of digitalization. Digitalization has changed the world much more than anyone imagined. Secondly, because digitalization has changed the world, it has also changed the customer. Thirdly, the speed of this change is staggering – something else that Dimon failed to appreciate at first. He knew that things would change, but thought the bank would have time to deal with it, perhaps until 2020, or 2025, or even 2030. Then he suddenly realized that

'IF THE CEO OF AMERICA'S
LARGEST BANK LOSES
SLEEP AT NIGHT BECAUSE
OF START-UPS, CLEARLY
SOMETHING IS AWRY.'

things were moving much faster than he anticipated. It is a lesson from which we can all learn.

You might wonder how it is possible that the radar at the top of such a major bank failed to pick up this threat for so long. How could its settings be so wrong? Are they still wrong? If you make a wrong assessment of important evolutions, this is usually because you are looking at reality through the wrong lens. Your way of thinking and your frames of reference are not fit for purpose. Perhaps your lens is too strong, so that you no longer see what is staring you in the face. You make poor judgements based on inadequate information and before you know it the world has been turned upside down, leaving you adrift in a new, volatile, uncertain, complex and ambiguous sea.

Technology rules

Whoever wants to look forward into the future should focus their attention on the forces that will determine the environment. You must map out those forces, choose the ones you think will be decisive and keep a close watch on how they develop. At the same time, you should train your antenna to pick up relevant signals that will allow you to interpret facts and formulate opinions.

The classic point of view is that the interplay of forces in our external environment can best be assessed in a PEST analysis. PEST stands for Political, Environmental, Social and Technological. Four major forces. Today, however, one of those four overshadows all the others: technology. Goodbye PEST analysis! Hello T analysis! Technology dominates. Moreover, technology also shakes up all the other key indicators in society. Technology makes it possible for companies to launch completely new business models onto the market. Technology turns those markets inside out and upside down. Technology empowers the modern consumer, leading for demands to even more change and innovation.

You could, of course, ask: 'So what's new about that? People who were used to riding in horse-drawn carriages were probably also amazed when cars first began appearing on the roads a hundred or so years ago. And what about the first plane? Or the first radio, telephone or television? Or the first computer? Or rockets to the moon? There has always been new technology that turned the world upside down.' True – and with a little bit of luck those first cars of a century ago might even have been electric ones!

Far be it for me to plug the Porsche brand, but the first model designed by Ferdinand Porsche, powered by the Lohner-Porsche system, was a hybrid. That was back in 1898.[13] Remember that date for later. Until the end of the 1910s, the electric car was a commercially viable alternative for the petrol-driven models. There were even chains of battery-charging stations. But then came Henry Ford and the advent of mass production. Exit electric propulsion. Disruption is nothing new.

Pioneering projects and exponential change curves are inherent to every new and ground-breaking technology. However, the scale and the manner in which technology is changing our lives is much deeper and much more comprehensive than ever before. The number of levers activated by today's technology is without precedent in human history. Nor has its influence ever been so worldwide. Every sector of the economy has been shaken up almost simultaneously, so that markets have become fluid.

Consider, for example, P – the political force – and the way technology is starting to dominate it. Both for good and ill. Thanks to technology, everyone can now spread news, fake or otherwise. Thanks to technology, elections can be won or lost. Thanks to technology, things can become crystal clear or obscurely ambiguous. What started off as the 'Arab Spring' was made possible by technology in the hands of ordinary people: the smartphone and social media. Nowadays, of course, the opposite is also true: politicians use technology to control (or at least influence) what people think and do. Instead of reading the paper and reacting to yesterday's news, we are now bombarded with updates almost 24/7. Today's politicians give instant comments on everything they do. But this can often muddy the waters, rather than making them clearer. Look, for example, at the role played by (fake) internet posts and social media during the previous American elections. And look at President Trump's favourite means of communication. To everyone's amazement, the American people elected a president who, according to the algorithms of the political pundits, had no chance of winning. Predictions for the national elections in France and the Netherlands were similarly wide of the mark. Every fake or genuine post and every fake or genuine opinion poll can spark off a popular counter-reaction on social media – which, as already said, can be for good or ill.

'NEVER BEFORE HAS THE IMPACT OF TECHNOLOGICAL CHANGE BEEN AS SWIFT AND AS FAR-REACHING AS IT IS TODAY.'

(Stop the presses!)

Literally. While I was reading the first printer's proof of what you are now reading, news started to come in about the Facebook leaks and the role of Cambridge Analytica.

In future, this will be seen as a historic moment. It reveals to the glare of public scrutiny for the very first time the influence of social media and data mining in combination with smart algorithms in a manner that is highly questionable, to say the least. In fact, it not only smells fishy – it stinks. A few weeks ago, I gave a keynote at the ABN-Amro tennis tournament in Rotterdam. The room was full of Dutch entrepreneurs. The speaker before me was Alex Nix, the CEO of Cambridge Analytica. He talked proudly (and a little condescendingly) about how his company had won the American elections for President Trump and how he had used the profiles of American electors 'acquired' by the company (and we now know exactly how this was done) to approach each individual elector in the best possible personalized way, using the right words and the right arguments.

Without literally saying so, he clearly hinted that they just looked at people's personal preferences and said that Trump supported the same opinions – even if it was not true. In this way, the individual electors were made to feel that Trump was his or her candidate. And indeed, many Trump voters still have a strong feeling that 'they' are running the country, because they believe that the man in the White House listens to them. In other words, above the line Trump said that he was going to break with political conventions, while below the line he let every voter decide for themselves how they would want this translated into practice for him or her, and consequently Trump would confirm these feelings. As a result, big data and smart algorithms were able to hijack the principles on which democracy is based. I will get back to this later on. Put simply, democracy was designed in and for a world that is very different from the world we live in today. What Cambridge Analytica did is to make clever use of new means and methods in a context that is not designed to cope with them and therefore has insufficient experience to detect possible 'deceit', let alone put a stop to it. It is like mechanical doping in cycle racing: an invisible electric motor built into the bike frame gives a bit of extra power at just the right moment without anyone else – well, almost anyone else – knowing what is happening.

While Nix was talking, you could sense the atmosphere in the room becoming uncomfortable: lots of whispered comments, shuffling of papers and embarrassed shifting in chairs. People were shocked by what he was saying. Not that he was aware of it. At the end of his speech he asked how many of the entrepreneurs present were interested in learning more about CA and maybe doing business with them. It was then his turn to be shocked – at the almost total lack of response.

Modern technology is also very close to consumers. As a result, it strongly influences their patterns of expectation: what they want, how they want it, where and when. Consider, for example, the environment. We are becoming increasingly aware of the impact we are having on our surroundings. We are better informed and more quickly informed about these matters than ever before. Every attack on the environment is magnified by the megaphone of social media until it becomes a scandal. We are constantly and increasingly being triggered to use less electricity, eat less meat, leave the car in the garage (or sell it altogether), etc. Ten years ago, the 'dieselgate' of Volkswagen could have been covered up quite easily. Today, that would be unthinkable – and impossible. We now realize that we are capable of destroying the environment with our old technology and that consequently we need new technological innovations to save the planet. The central store of knowledge about the environmental impact of humans has become a widely distributed opinion.

Describing the influence of T on our social behaviour is like kicking in an open door. Online and social media are here to stay. Life without them is now almost inconceivable. Never before have people allowed technology to play such a big part in their daily existence. The world is an open network in which everyone can play a role, everyone can have an opinion and everyone has created their own virtual personality. And these open networks play by different rules than the traditional markets: they are faster, less predictable and ruthless. The 'truth' – and what it means – is now shared among millions of different people. Opinion can no longer be directed centrally. One of the consequences of this is that lobby groups have lost much of their power.

In fact, open networks have completely overturned the general balance of power between organizations and their customers. Nowadays, if you have a good idea, you can easily build an online platform that wipes an established business model off the map. Never before have there been so many software coders who are using technology to change the world and challenge the existing order. All they need is a computer and an internet connection.

'NEVER BEFORE HAVE THERE BEEN SO MANY YOUNG SOFTWARE CODERS WHO ARE USING TECHNOLOGY TO CHANGE THE WORLD AND CHALLENGE THE EXISTING ORDER.'

Forget the word 'digital'. Digital is the new normal. If you use the adjective 'digital', you simply show that you are already out of date. The world is digitalized and customers are digitalized. Digital technology is embedded everywhere. Everything that can be done by software will be done by software. Why? Because software is faster than people, uses fewer resources and eliminates several expensive intermediary steps in the chain of any process. You can also forget the word 'online'. In the near future, everyone and everything will be 'online'. You can add 'mobile' to your list as well. Nowadays, the whole world is mobile. 'Connected' can likewise be consigned to the dustbin. Before long, everyone and everything will be connected to everyone and everything.

In other words, it is no longer about digital, online, mobile or connected. It is about the role that you want to play as a company in this new world, the world in which the customer has seized all the power. It is about your relevance for this empowered customer. Companies need to keep up with the new technological cloud. In this sense, evolution means genuinely adjusting and integrating into the new environment. Your commitment has to be 100%. You are not just changing your diet; you are changing your entire way of life.

Many companies exhaust their resources in an attempt to develop a digital strategy. They invest heavily. But they invest in the wrong things. Managers often think that developing a digital strategy is simply a matter of digitalizing your existing business model. That is exactly what you should not do. It just does not work. Digitalizing what you already do means that you already have a strategy, to which you now want to add a digital layer. This is not the kind of transformation that is necessary if you want to succeed. So don't talk about a digital strategy. This tells people that you are going to carry on doing the same old things, but have simply thrown in a bit of extra technology to make it look 'new'. What companies need to do is to dream up and roll out an alternative strategy that is adjusted to the demands of the digital world. In short, you must re-invent your business model.

'IT'S NOT ABOUT A DIGITAL STRATEGY. IT'S ABOUT A STRATEGY FOR THE DIGITAL WORLD.'

Shark's fin

In the past, thinking ahead strategically was a relatively simple matter. You looked at the existing market, at the available technology and at current customer behaviour. Subsequently you simply extrapolated this to whatever period seemed appropriate, using growth figures and market reports to back up your case. It was pretty easy to knock up a five year plan, complete with suitable milestones, perhaps while lying alongside the swimming pool during your summer holidays. Every so often you might have to update the plan with new figures – but that was all you had to do. In the meantime, everyone in the company could switch to execution mode: start, hold, repeat. This was enough, because although the world was still subject to change, it changed at a relatively slow pace. Even if a high wave of change rose threateningly on the horizon, it was still visible from such a long way off and approached so sluggishly that there was always plenty of time to see how other companies and consumers were reacting, so that you could adjust accordingly.

At business school, we learned that the process by which consumers pick up new innovations progresses in accordance with a Gauss curve. This curve reflects the idea that companies have ample time to see what early adopters and the early majority do with the products launched by the innovators. By watching and waiting, it is possible to avoid the mistakes and the high costs of these pioneers. As a smart follower, you can learn from the errors of others and amend your own approach in a way that is guaranteed to appeal to the large majority of customers: adjust, hold, repeat.

This kind of slow innovation no longer exists. Today's innovation is very different. But how exactly does it work? First, there are a number of early signals or early hiccups. These suggest that something new is on the way. Someone is offering something that is completely different. These early hiccups are picked up by the trendsetters. Or perhaps they are not. Some early hiccups come to nothing. However, others attract growing interest. After a succession of early hiccups, an early warning bell starts to ring.

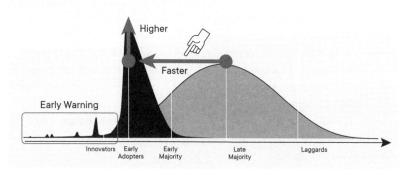

Big Bang Disruption / Larry Downes & Paul Nunes
The way a consumer picks up on innovation: what we learnt at school against how the real innovators do it today – Gauss versus the shark's fin.

As soon as the new innovation become reasonably well established and is picked up by the 'average' customer, things move into overdrive. The different waves of adoption come faster and faster, and have much more impact than was previously the case. In fact, the impact increases exponentially, producing a sharp peak: the shark's fin curve.

Typical to any and thus also this exponential curve: it takes progressively less time to produce the same degree of change. As a result, adjusting to this change is not easy, because the associated technology is also changing at an astonishing pace. Companies understandably want to keep ahead of their rivals, which heightens the urgency for developing new technological solutions and new plans.

It is interesting to take a brief step back in time to look at the early signals given by some recent innovations. Regard it as a useful exercise to sharpen up your ability to spot new early warnings today. For example, the introduction of Google Glass was an early hiccup to show that virtual reality was on the way. So too was the advent of the large and somewhat cumbersome 3D-glasses. Both these innovations were saying 'the technology exists' and 'the application for its use exists'. It was not until iPhone's VR programme was launched, that the technology made its breakthrough. There are currently thousands of companies that want to build up their business around virtual applications. They are all looking for the right interface, the right form and the right connectivity. And they are all influencing each other.

In other words, change occurs in a diverse and often ambiguous manner under the surface. True, some of the connections might be visible. But a lot of them are not. This diversity and ambiguity results from the fact that today's innovators play by different rules than the established order. The innovators build mirror-images of existing business models. They re-invent these models by mirroring what already is, whilst at the same time giving it a new and completely different interpretation, which they then implement in accordance with a new set of digital laws, placing the modern customer firmly in the central position. As said, this customer has become highly demanding: he wants everything to be easier, friendlier, simpler, faster, freer and more respectful. What is more, he also wants to be involved. The first consumers who gravitate towards this parallel mirror-model become the marketers of change.

This new, alternative, mirror-image offer remains hidden from the established order for quite some time, because they continue to have blind faith in classic KPIs, which are not suited to take account of the new rules of the game. It is only when the innovative offers starts 'infecting' one customer after another, almost like a contagious disease, that the truth of what is really happening finally dawns. Mind you, once consumers have tasted the sweet fruits of the new innovation – ease, speed, convenience, etc. – they will not be satisfied with anything less. It is as if a new world has opened up to them and they are quick to recommend it to other consumers. This leads to a chain reaction, in which a whole series of other 'worlds', both great and small, are turned upside down: not just the world of the customer, but also the worlds of production, media, politics, work …

The technological cloud, with its potential for generating exponential effects, is the facilitator of change. So, too, are the disruptive business models, which develop alongside existing models as their parallel reflection. But of the two, it is the technology that most forcefully drives the change process. It is technology that enables completely new business models to be created. Only by allowing the consumer to take on the role of marketer, facilitator or even supplier of infrastructure, can these models truly shine. Innovators are able to make use of things that are already present in the market (and therefore familiar to the consumer), they can quickly ratchet up the speed of the innovation process. One cog turns the other. The changing of the world is driven by the interaction of new technology, new and mirror-imaged business models, and new consumers who help to market the change.

The Chicxulub meteor

Nature doesn't care whether you survive as an individual or not. But the survival of life in general is a different matter. And to ensure that life in general survives, it is necessary for that life to evolve. Species need to develop and improve if they wish to continue their existence. They must make themselves attractive enough for long enough, so that they can procreate as much as possible. The more offspring they have, the greater the likelihood that some of them will make it through to the next generation. In this way, sometimes a species is given long enough to adjust to changing circumstances. And sometimes it isn't. Too bad.

Consider, for example, the extinction of the dinosaurs some 65 to 66 million years ago, in the time between the Cretaceous and Tertiary periods. Scientists still don't really know for sure what happened, but within ten years these giants of the prehistoric world had vanished from the face of the earth. It seems certain that the impact of a huge meteor in what is now Yucatan (Mexico) had something to do with it. The Chicxulub crater is 180 kilometres wide.[14] All the debris that its impact blasted into the stratosphere blocked out the sun, so that the climate cooled and became drier. The greater the distance from the equator, the more extreme the cold and the drought. And the greater the number of life forms that perished.

If the meteor had deviated from its course by just a single degree, then our world today would be a very different place. Perhaps the meteor would have missed the earth completely. Or maybe it could have landed somewhere other than the Yucatan, at a place that would have blown less material into the atmosphere, allowing more sunlight to reach the surface and warm the planet.[15]

According to one theory, it was clouds of sulphate that blocked out the sun. According to another, the meteor landed in the middle of giant oil fields, which burst into flames and filled the skies with smoke.[16] But they remain just theories; no-one really knows.   Although the second theory might explain why smaller dinosaurs, like the prehistoric species of crocodile and their other small crawling, walking and flying relatives, survived. Which also explains why we are still able to eat chicken today – and occasionally crocodile.

'THE LAST OF THE GREAT DINOSAURS NEVER REGARDED THE FIRST MAMMALS (A FORM OF RAT) AS DISRUPTORS.'

The last of the great dinosaurs never regarded the first mammals (a form of rat) as disruptors. For one thing, their walnut-sized brains wouldn't have known what the word means. The point is: the first mammals survived the impact of the meteor and the aftermath, whereas the dinosaurs did not. This was not because the mammals were bigger or stronger. It was because they were more fitted. They could breed more quickly and adjust more quickly to the dramatically changed circumstances. For one thing, they could generate their own heat. It is probable as well that they were less dependent on specific sources of food. Or perhaps they learnt the secret of storing food and of hibernating, like their later descendants, the hamsters. In contrast, the massive, slow dinosaurs had to spend a great deal of time and energy simply trying to maintain their own huge size, never mind breeding new generations of baby dinosaurs.

To exist, you need a degree of order. To survive, you need a degree of resilience. A very high degree of resilience. According to my friend and biologist Leen Gorissen, there are only three strategies to make it through a period of disruption unscathed. You can implement one strategy or combine them.

The first one is the strategy of the perfect design. This perfect design, with thanks to your parents, allows you to overcome all problems and survive any setbacks. The shark is a good example. So is the crocodile. And the scorpion. Their design has hardly changed across millions of years, because at some point it reached a state of perfection that required no further evolution. It was perfectly adapted to meet all the challenges of its environment, no matter how hard they might be. Crocodiles can survive without water for years. Sharks can endlessly regenerate their own teeth. The scorpion can even cope with serious doses of nuclear radiation.

The sea turtle is another species with perfect design. How do we know? Because it has survived in the hostile environment of the sea for more than a hundred million years. Even so, the sea turtle is starting to find things difficult, because the most destructive of all creatures – man – is now interfering with its habitat. Sometimes nature can make a species so perfect that it forgets there was ever such a thing as evolution. Sea turtles lay their eggs on the beach where they were born, preferably in clean sand. But clean beaches are getting hard to find. Rubbish, light pollution and human presence have all contributed to a significant fall in the number of turtle nests.[17] Even more, the baby turtles need to wait until there is a full moon above the sea before hatching. Their instinct is programmed to use the moon's light to find their way to the water. However, nowadays, so much artificial inland light pollutes the beaches, that they end up going the wrong way. Often with fatal consequences.

This highlights an interesting point about perfect design: you can never really be sure that it is indeed 100% perfect. You may think you are the best version of what you can be – but are you? All you know is that this design has served you well – very well – up until now. It has allowed you not only to survive but even to flourish in your chosen environment. However, will it still do the same tomorrow? No matter how sharp and how numerous their teeth are, even sharks are finding it difficult to cope with the huge amounts of plastic pollution in our (or rather, their) oceans. Companies like Nokia and Kodak no doubt also thought that their devices were perfectly designed and would stand the test of time – and we all know what happened to them. Today, it is probably fair to say that the iPhone has a perfect design – but for how long?

Of course, as a species you could always opt for the second survival strategy: being smart and learning how to adapt your behaviour. The fox' natural biotope is being reduced systematically, but they are clever enough to extend their radius of action to a non-natural biotope: the city. Stone martens are another good example. They have learnt to love our attics and the warm engines of our motor cars standing on our driveways. Not to mention our chicken coops and rubbish bins. And what can we say about the falcon? These birds of prey are also starting to appear in the city. The reasons are not hard to find. Cities have a plentiful supply of plump, juicy pigeons and also plenty of tall buildings from which to spot their prey.

If all else fails, there is always option number three: increase your rate of reproduction, by increasing both the speed of the cycle and the number of offspring per litter. The more of you there are, the more chance that some of you will survive. At the same time, genetic drift will ensure that over time your species becomes more suited to survival. Rats use very little energy to produce large numbers of little rats. Elephants use a huge amount of effort to produce relatively few baby elephants. Man will never be able to exterminate rats entirely, no matter how hard he tries, but he is almost certain to hunt elephants to extinction.

There is, however, a fourth and final way to maximize your chances of survival: make use of the self-sustaining power of your network. Learn to swim in shoals. Or hunt in packs. Or fly in swarms. Sardines do so, as do wolves. And so do starlings. Or you can live in a colony, like termites and ants. Intelligence and innovation are generated by the combined power of the network, not by the efforts of individuals. With this option, survival of the species overrides the interests of the individual. Which makes sense: without the school, swarm or colony, the individual's chances of survival are zero anyway.

Genetic drift

The story of the dinosaurs teaches us a lot. First: shit happens – and usually when you least expect it. So it's a good idea to take account of the possibility of exceptional hiccups that might have an impact on your survival chances. Second: being big is not always an advantage. As a big company, you are inclined to spend time and money simply on maintaining your size. However, size inherently means complexity, whereas the lines of communication in smaller firms are shorter, so that these firms are often more alert and can react faster. Third: to survive, you need to be able to change your DNA (your values, habits and business model) with adequate speed, so that you can produce better future generations in shorter iterations.

If you translate these ideas to a sector or company, you can see that this effectively means they need to re-invent themselves in the shortest possible time through a process of genetic drift in their DNA, if they wish to survive as a 'species' across the different mutations of business models. Of course, you can always just trust to luck and hope that things will turn out alright for you in the new environment, but as a strategy that is about as risky as it gets.

The world of nature can teach enterprises and entrepreneurs a lot. You can compare a company with an organism, which needs to make its products as attractive as possible, so that it can find the maximum number of partners to keep itself alive in and through future generations. At the same time, the individual company is involved in a battle with all the other individual organisms (other companies) for the necessary nourishment (market) and sexual response (customers). Within the species, evolution will operate in its different random ways. There will be pioneers who adjust their DNA to the new circumstances and there will be laggards who do so more slowly or not at all. And there will be those who kick-start their genetic drift. These are the innovators and the disruptors, and they will run off with the biggest share of both market and customers. Their genetic drift will ensure that their company survives as a species.

In practical terms, It is about experimenting with new business models and products, giving them a chance to show what they can do and choosing between the things that work and the things that don't, so that you can bring the most likely successes to market as quickly as possible. It is these successful variants that ensure your continued existence.

In an environment where everything is changing quickly, having a fast reproductive cycle is crucial. For this, you need a huge amount of data. The better you are able to read the 'flow of information'[18] in your environment and re-interpret your DNA in light of this data, 'cross-breeding' it with new building blocks in new business models, the greater the likelihood that you will achieve an excellent fit with the environment in terms of your reproduction.

'COMPANIES TODAY HAVE LITTLE OPTION BUT TO EMBRACE THE NETWORK IDEA.'

In this battle for survival, you can (and should) make use of the strength of your network. Companies today have little option but to embrace the network idea. Four different types of network spring to mind:
- an innovation network that allows companies to share knowledge quicker and more easily, making making faster innovation possible and allowing more room for creativity.[19]

- an internal cultural network that provides social cohesion and good internal collaboration (culture);[20]
- a hierarchical network that sets out the roles to be played by everyone (control);[21]
- an external cultural network; in the past, in more rigid times, this would have been the safe network of a sector; nowadays, it is the network that synchronizes the company's evolution with the evolution of the customer in the external world (evolution).

A modern network is always open. In other words, the shape and form of the network itself reflects the fluidity of the circumstances. The modern network also evolves, because it also runs synchronously with other networks.

As mankind, we have one huge advantage over other animals. It is this advantage which explains why humans have been so successful as a species. Historian Yuval Noah Harari wrote about it in his book *Sapiens*.[22] Harari lectures in history at the Hebrew University of Jerusalem. What distinguishes us from the other animals, he says, is our ability to create imaginary realities and entities. By imagining a reality and adding meaning to it, we are able to work towards that reality with purpose and desire. And if we don't like the structure of our colony or swarm, we can change it. 'We can work flexibly with an infinite number of strangers, because we alone, among all the animals on the planet, are capable of creating and believing in fictional stories,' dixit Harari in a TED-talk.[23] 'As long as everyone believes in the same fiction, everyone will follow and obey the same rules and the same values. All other animals use their communication systems to do no more than describe reality. '

'FROM THE FUTURE WE CAN CREATE THINGS IN THE PRESENT.' Animals are trapped in the here and now. As humans, we can imagine a future and, based on that fiction, create a new reality in the present. That is why it is so important to dare to see evolution for what it is, as the way in which things can change and progress. And once you have made this recognition, you must do something about it.

Learning to see evolution

We humans are not very good at comprehending time. We forget things, especially dates. However, the 30th of April 1993 is a date worth remembering. That was the date on which the CERN first made web technology public. CERN stands for *Conseil Européen pour la Recherche Nucléaire* or European Council for Nuclear Research. Until then, the internet had been used exclusively for military purposes. One of the founding fathers of the public internet is Belgian computer scientist Robert Cailliau, who worked for the CERN in Geneva. In collaboration with the German research institute *Fraunhofer-Gesellschaft*, he set up the web project of the European Commission for the dissemination of information in Europe. In December 1993, Cailliau and CERN announced that the first international www-conference would be held in May of the following year. Only a small group of specialists knew what they were talking about. Very few people had ever even heard of the internet. As a result, only 380 people actually turned up for the conference.[24] In 1991, there was just a single website. By 1992, there were ten. By 1993, one hundred and thirty. Compare this to the almost unbelievable state of affairs with the blockchain anno 2015, just two decades later.

In other words, the internet is little more than 20 years old. Or should I say 'scarcely'? At the start of the 1990s, I was a young manager (back in those days, a thirty-year-old sales manager was regarded as being very young indeed!). At the time, I did not understand the internet. It made its entrance into my life, but I wasn't particularly impressed. It took minutes to load a webpage and often the result of all that waiting was just a logo and a telephone number. You were better off with the yellow pages – or so I thought. However, you had to go on the internet if you wanted to be seen as 'advanced' and so our company did. And there was indeed something 'exciting' and 'special' about the early pioneering days of internet. A single 'pc with internet connection' stood in the centre of the office. In the best offices there might even have been a second one, with – if you were very lucky – a colour screen. Usually, these luxuries were given their own separate area. This meant that if, for whatever bizarre reason, you wanted to 'go on the internet', everyone else in the office could see you and wanted to know what on earth you were doing. As a result, the internet became a source of rumour and gossip. 'John was on the internet for hours today.' 'Yes, I saw. I wonder what he was up to?' There were also problems if you wanted to 'surf' at home: the rest of the family couldn't use the telephone for hours!

Once the technology was made public, its growth was explosive. The hundred websites at the end of 1993 became 2,738 websites by the end of 1994. Making a web page quickly became easier and easier. The first browsers began to appear. The term 'web interface' was heard for the first time and the first online shops launched their products with an online order form.

Inevitably, the first signs of competition soon followed. In 1996, there was a major browser war between Internet Explorer and Netscape Navigator. By 1997, there was a kind of soap bubble developing: just add '.com' after your company name and the money would start rolling in, almost by itself!

In the meantime, I was trying to survive in the carpet industry, where the biggest monster we had to fight was the accumulated heritage of years of unbridled and short-sighted expansion. Back then, the carpet sector was plagued by over-production, made worse by the power of the retailers and the effects of price competition. Worst of all, we were losing customers in droves. It was in this 'scorched earth' setting that I tried to do my job for the company and make a career. In contrast to what people were saying, the money did not come rolling in of its own accord. We had internet, but I didn't understand how to use it. I saw lots of web pages and occasionally some e-commerce, but I remember thinking at the time that these were some kind of mail order companies…

It was not until 1998 that I went to senior management and suggested that perhaps we should try building our own website. Nowadays, we are all familiar with the old maxim that eighty percent of business is realized by just twenty percent of customers, so it is better to cut off that expensive long tail. I, however, pleaded to keep the tail and to service it with what I called 'digital delight'. What I was suggesting was something similar to what internet banking was then doing: using online facilities to offer services to customers who were too small and therefore too costly to service in any other 'normal' way. To be honest, that was the full extent of my 'digital strategy'. I was laughed out of the boardroom.

Even though I was proud of these insights and notwithstanding the resistance I had from the board, I still had no idea of just how dramatically the internet would change the world. In 1998, there were 2.4 million websites. Amazon had been in existence for three years. In 1999, a certain Alexander Klöpping built the first website for our carpet company. The name Google was also starting to be heard with increasing frequency and the idea for Bol.com was starting to ripen in the mind of a young consultant called Daniel Ropers.

In 1998, I still failed to realize that developing a business model for the internet world has nothing to do with digital strategy; in other words, with a strategy that you develop alongside your 'analogue' strategy like some kind of functional growth, a utilitarian addition, an addendum that serves to make everything that already exists just a little bit better. However, you didn't need a digital strategy; what you needed was a strategy to deal with the digital world that was starting to emerge. The entrepreneurs who understood this at the right moment, who recognized what a strategy for the digital world could mean and translated those insights consistently into an offer and a business model – these are the people we look up to today.

In the beginning, there was blockchain

Today is 16 January 2018. It is exactly four minutes past midday. There are now 1,319,993,083 websites online. No, I am lying. Before I have even completing typing this figure, the number has increased to 1,319,993,440. Check out www.internetstats.com if you want to find out things like the number of internet users, smartphone sales, Google searches and other digital trivia, such as the number of hacks and sent e-mails. The internet has gradually worked its way into our lives and suddenly everyone and everything is online. Without the internet, the world would no longer be able to function. Being online is now almost as important as breathing! And if I see the evolution the world and our behaviour online has made during the past 20 years, then this inspires me to think ahead to the changes that today are still hidden in the blockchain …

Blockchain makes many of the intermediary links in the verification chain of data details unnecessary. More and more authorities, governmental and otherwise, are coming to the conclusion that blockchain, the accounting peer-to-peer data journal that belongs to everyone and no-one, represents a significant political challenge in the years ahead. The Netherlands says that it wants to become the first blockchain government. Estonia believes that it already is. Since 2012 blockchain has been operational in the country's health, legal, legislative, security and economic coding systems and the Estonian government hopes to extend its blockchain applications to other areas, such as personal medicine and cyber security.[25]

If you told people twenty years ago that we would come to rely on an online encyclopaedia written by ourselves, people would probably have said: 'pull the other one'. I also knew people who said: 'Buy things on the internet? Never! And use Facebook? You must be joking!' Yet little by little we modify our attitude towards the things that confront us in our ever-changing world. And by looking in the rear-view mirror of history, we can often identify the exact tipping point in our perception. Before we know it, that moment arrives. Suddenly, we see the world differently and we treat its players differently. And once we have reached this tipping point, we stay tipped.

'ALMOST NO-ONE UNDERSTANDS BLOCKCHAIN, BUT THAT WAS ALSO TRUE FOR THE INTERNET IN THE EARLY DAYS.'

Blockchain still seems like a strange technology at present, so perhaps it is wise to have our suspicions about it. After all, almost no-one understands blockchain. Those who do, have not yet found a way to make it comprehensible to the others so far. Then again, that was also true for the internet in the early days. 'We are cautious about it in the short term. However, you have to temper that with the idea that every new technology is going to be like that in the beginning,' said Peter Smith, the CEO of Blockchain at the Fortune Brainstorm Tech Conference in 2017.[26] Much the same is true for artificial intelligence. This is another technology that seems slightly weird to many people, just like the internet did back in 1993. But as soon as the technology makes our lives faster, easier, simpler and more pleasant, we will be quick to embrace it.

It may seem as though we eventually integrate new elements into our lives, but actually it is the other way around. It is us who integrate ourselves into the new world. And for people who can find a place in this upside down world, it quickly becomes their new standard. The old world suddenly seems too slow, too complicated and too unfriendly. Once we are settled into the new world, we will never want to go back to our old ways. This is the 'New Normal', about which technology entrepreneur Peter Hinssen already wrote a book in 2013, a book you must read.

The upside down world

In 2013, I visited the Googleplex in Silicon Valley. While I was there, I saw the prototype of Google's self-driving car. Not on the public road, but on the Google campus. At the time, Google thought that the first self-driving cars would appear on our roads sometime around 2030. However, by the time we visited Silicon Valley again in 2015, the first Google Cars were already being tested on America's highways and byways. In other words, the year 2030 is closer than you think, even for a forward-looking company like Google. In fact, 2030 is often already here today! Google has since withdrawn from the race to mass produce self-driving cars, but continues to develop the software that will be needed by other manufacturers. By 2015, Google's self-driving cars had ridden some four million kilometres on public roads and had only been involved in two accidents. In both cases, it involved a human driver crashing into the Google car. All that is now standing in the way of the further rolling out of these cars on a large scale is the requisite legislation.

Things are moving fast. Lyft, Uber and Waymo, a subsidiary of Alphabet, the umbrella organization above Google, are battling against each other and the other major players, like Tesla, to win the race to be the first to bring self-driving cars to the commercial market. GM recently announced (12 January 2018) that it plans to launch an electric Chevrolet without a steering wheel or foot pedals. They intend to start mass production in... 2019. Companies still talk about a world in change. But perhaps the time has come to realize that we should be talking about a change of world. What (primarily large) companies fail (or do not want) to understand is that exponential evolutions are no longer a matter of new production factors or greater efficiency. The forces at work in today's markets make entire business models unnecessary and obsolete.

We are living at a crossroads, our own Copernican revolution that will turn entire worlds upside down. I deliberately choose to write 'worlds' in the plural form, because it is not only the world of 'this politician' or 'that company' which will be turned upside down. All our micro and macro-worlds, whether social, geopolitical, economic or technological, will be shaken up in a way we have never experienced before.

Companies are still insufficiently aware that we have reached this societal turning point. They know that technology is changing. They see the emergence of new competitors. They feel the impact of additional legislation. However, they fail to realize that these are signals of underlying forces that are revolutionizing the world. And so they fail to appreciate – and extrapolate from – the coherence of these forces. They neglect to change their world view – the way they look at the world – with sufficient thoroughness. They fail to notice that their model is being undermined by newcomers, who seem to be offering the same as they are, but are, in fact, doing something radically different. They completely overlook the fact that customer and market behaviour have been transformed in recent years. Power is now in the hands of consumers and they make decisions very differently than in the past. Things used to be so well-ordered, so neatly arranged, so familiar. Not anymore. If you recognize this attitude in your own environment, it is time to give the people around you a wake-up call.

History is full of turning points where everything that was once familiar suddenly seems changed, where top becomes bottom and bottom becomes top. The main difference today is that the speed of impact of this process is greater than it has ever been before. Change hits us like a bolt from the blue and before we know it has become irreversible: BOOM! Overnight, we need to think in terms of a new paradigm.

'PERHAPS THE TIME HAS COME TO REALIZE THAT WE SHOULD BE TALKING ABOUT A CHANGE OF WORLD. '

These turning points have a number of common characteristics that can help you to identify them. They are always preceded by a period of fluidity and transformation. The dice are already rolling. However, at a given moment the dice finally come to a stop and change kicks in. From this moment on, the old ways cease to exist and are replaced by a new reality that turns everything upside down. Perhaps not unsurprisingly, this is followed by a period of turmoil and unrest. The old rules no longer apply, but the new rules are not yet sufficiently well-known or accepted. A turning point requires people to think and act in new ways – and that is never easy. You can think of it as the need to make a jump. There are some people who make this necessary jump. There are others who cannot understand why people are jumping at all. There are yet others who want to make the jump but do not have the courage to do it. Finally, there is the group who are simply unwilling or unable to jump.

Another key characteristic is that important turning points are never initiated by the existing order. People who owe their power to the 'old' view of the world have nothing to gain by turning this world upside down. As a result, the 'old guard' will fiercely resist any attempt at change by persisting to apply prevailing rules and regulations. When this fails, they will continue to deny the existence of change for as long as they possibly can. In the end, this usually results in bloodshed of one kind or another. Most people will fight to try and ensure the survival of their own view of the world. Those on the losing side of this battle often run away from the reality of their defeat, burying their head in the sand in the hope that things will 'somehow' get better. You often see this kind of thing in the business world. Some companies attempt to ride roughshod over the new trends; others simply ignore them until it is too late, wrongly believing that their position is invincible.

These are moments when for one side their world collapses, while for the other side a whole new world of possibilities opens up. Our common past is full of instances where new ideas, new inventions, wars and revolutions have created a completely new way of looking at – and responding to – the world around us. The familiar way of doing things comes to an end, giving way to radical and dynamic alternatives. The old is dead; long live the new! Such moments do not always need to happen on a grand scale. A series of smaller turning points can sometimes be enough to trigger huge change. However, the reverse can also be true. The effects of major turning points often continue to filter down for many years as a number of smaller but nonetheless significant developments.

Turing points always provide an 'aha!' experience, the feeling that things will never be the same again. You can recognize this from the look of disbelief or fury in the eyes of those who thought they had everything under control and from the outbursts of joy from life's underdogs, daredevils and revolutionaries. You can see it in the powerlessness of the former arbiters of 'truth' to come to terms with the new disruptive forces that are sweeping them away. Faced with this incomprehensible topsy-turvy situation, their only options are to surrender, run or fight. But it makes no difference: their defeat is certain. However, this does not mean that every turning point is necessarily all good. There will certainly be good bits, but bad bits as well. Every action leads to a reaction.

In *Homo Deus* Yuval Harari describes this kind of turning-point moment without using those words. He refers to the last-ever speech by the Rumanian dictator, Nicolae Ceaușescu, which you can still watch on YouTube. Ceaușescu mumbles on with his speech until someone in the audience suddenly shouts out (in Rumanian, of course!): 'Boo! Down with C!' Within seconds, everyone is joining in: 'Boo! Down with C!' You can see that Ceaușescu doesn't understand what is going on. He simply stares in puzzlement at the increasingly angry crowd. In that single second, writes Harari, his world collapses around him.[27]

This was a classic example: left against right and vice versa, with an equally classic top-down pattern. Nowadays, however, more and more patterns of this kind are starting at the base and working their way upwards. The victory of the Five Star Movement in the March 2018 elections in Italy is good example of this type of bottom-up turning point in a political context. The Movement came from nowhere. It simply began as a group of ordinary people getting together because they were not happy with the way things were going in their country. Much to the amazement of the political pundits (and many of its own members), the group continued to grow until it first became a movement and later crystallized into a party. It was able to unite people around themes that are not necessarily political per se and which therefore do not fit neatly into the traditional party political structure. At the time of writing, we do not yet know how the political adventure of the Five Star Movement is likely to end. It is perfectly possible that another 'face-lifted' player will appear on the scene to upset the democratic balance even more.

The evolution and openness of the media have played a crucial role in the dissemination of turning points. Copernicus waited for decades before he dared to publish *Revolutionibus Orbium Coelestium* in 1543, his own turning-point moment. And it still took weeks for news of Napoleon's defeat at Waterloo to spread across Europe in 1815. By the time the Wright brothers made the first powered flight in 1903, the event was able to be captured on photo and printed in the newspapers the next day. And by the time Neil Armstrong took man's first step on the moon in 1969, millions were watching the event live on their own television sets at home. The fall of the Berlin Wall, the attack on the twin towers at the World Trade Centre... These are all events with a very clear 'before' and 'after'. The difference lies in the speed with which we are able to observe and assimilate such events in the modern world. You can view today's turning points on our smartphone. And if, for whatever reason, you miss something, you can always find a blow-by-blow account on YouTube. We have become obsessed with the filming of our own turning points, both real and imagined.

Learning to look through the mirror

Whenever I visit The Hague, I always make time to pop in at the Escher Museum in The Palace. Maurits Cornelis Escher is famous for his drawings and woodcuts of never-ending staircases and impossible perspectives. In Escher's world everything looks familiar but nothing is what it seems. As the viewer, you are constantly thrown off balance. What appears to be the back is actually the front. And what looks like the top is really the bottom. And vice versa... Confused? That's hardly surprising: Escher plays with the shortcuts in your brain. You see things that are not there and fail to see the things that are. Mirror images become real figures before disappearing back among the mirrors. When, as a manager, you begin to realize that the reflected world has become reality, you are finally starting to think like Escher: you understand the need to add a new and unexpected dimension to whatever already exists.

Having said that, I must confess that when I first heard about the Ubers, Airbnbs and other disruptors of this world, I (like the vast majority of people) did not think they had anything special to offer. By the time Uber and Airbnb first started, back in 2008-2009, I had long since left the carpet industry and was helping businesses to develop better relations with their customers through the use of technology. As a result, I was on good terms with many of the top technology companies. When I first listened to the ever enthusiastic Steven Van Belleghem tell his exciting stories about the bold newcomers in Silicon Valley, my first reaction was one of 'yes, but'. It sounded too good to be true and all I could see was the potential problems and pitfalls. It was much the same on a later occasion, when I heard

Steven and Alexander Klöpping speak at a congress of CRM partners in Ede. They both talked passionately about Uber and Airbnb, almost as if companies of this kind were some new type of holy grail. However, I was still not convinced about the feasibility and, above all, the sustainability of their business model. Looking back, it is that 'yes, but' attitude that now so intrigues me. Why couldn't I see it? Or did I perhaps not want to see it?

I could see and understand the models. What I failed to see was the new context in which the models were being developed. I viewed the models through the lens of the old paradigm and, as a result, was unable to see what was staring me in the face. All I saw was an impossible Escher drawing. I listened to what was being said, but could not understand the language. What Airbnb and Uber did (and still do) is nothing more than take an existing business model and then reflect it in the mirror of an environment where digital laws hold sway.

Of course, I should have known. Every piece of valid scientific research starts with the setting of boundaries and a clarification of the initial position of the observer. However, I wasn't an observer. I was a participant in the old world, trapped in its outdated paradigms. I saw what I wanted to see and was unable to see what I did not understand. Or as the Dutch footballing genius and philosopher Johan Cruijff once put it: 'You can only see it when you understand it'. Which is true. But the opposite is true as well: you can only see and understand what you know and understand. If you do not know or expect something, you cannot see it coming – and therefore cannot understand it when it arrives. You cannot understand the upside down digital world with old-style insights, measuring instruments and logic. You can only understand it if you radically change your thinking and behaviour, by daring to turn your own familiar world upside down.

Force of habit and the fallacy of 'enough time'

Recently, I saw a striking poster for the fantastic science fiction horror series *Stranger Things*, one of the so-called Netflix Originals. In a flash, I also saw something that possibly even Netflix has not yet realized. *Stranger Things* is actually a parody (presumably unintentional) of the way Netflix itself has taken over the old world of film and television. I saw the old surface world and the new, upside-down-under-the-surface world. I saw a mirror image of something that is not there! I saw people living in the surface world who had no idea of the developments taking place beneath their feet. Until, that is,

Poster Stranger Things, Netflix

those developments are ready to break into that surface world, with all the unpleasant consequences this entails.

It continues to amaze me just how many companies still fail to fully grasp the impact and the possibilities offered by technology. They persist in seeing technology as a production factor. If they invest in it, they think exclusively in classic terms of increased efficiency. They believe that technology can give them a competitive advantage. In many cases, they regard digital applications as nothing more than an extra layer to be added on top of their existing structures and processes.

When companies of this kind say that they are 'going digital', what they actually mean is that they are going to do exactly the same as they have always done, only by digital means. And when they come to the conclusion that their familiar procedures no longer work, their only answer is to try and devise a new model whose sole purpose is to turn the clock back to the way things used to be. In other words, their playing field remains the same, even though the game itself has actually moved on by leaps and bounds. Too many companies persist in believing that they make the market. This fundamental opinion remains unaltered. Unfortunately, it is also fundamentally wrong! These companies are often obsessively occupied with digitalization, but all they are digitalizing are their old internal processes!

Our brain does not really help us when it comes to identifying new elements in our environment. It is happy with the familiar. Unless you make a conscious effort and actively train your mind to look out for things that deviate from the norm and from standard patterns of expectation, most innovations will pass under your radar. For this reason, it is useful to occasionally ask yourself whether what you see is really there and also whether there are things you are forgetting to see. The force of habit to see some things because they have always been there and not to see other things because they have never been there often combine to make people blind to the reality of the situation. If you keep telling the same story time after time and hear others repeating it, you eventually come to believe that it is the only good story. The gravitational pull of the familiar might just be enough to keep you upright, but it might just as easily pull you down. Managers need to learn to think upside down.

Another misleading psychological quirk of the company brain is to think that there is always enough time to adjust to developments taking place outside our market. Or we think that these developments are running par-

49

DISRUPTION IS NORMAL

allel to the market, like some kind of mirror image of our own business. This false logic further assumes that anything running parallel to our own course will, by definition, never be able to collide with us, so that it can be safely ignored. As a result, these 'novelties' are seen as something for others, for a sub-culture or a counterculture, or for a group of eccentric customers who per se want something 'different'.

Too many managers 'see nothing for us' in Uber, Twitter, Facebook, Pinterest, Dropbox, Lending Club, Instagram, Evernote, Nest, Waze, etc. They think they do not need to do anything, because they cannot see any useful benefit. They continue to view these mavericks from another dimension from the narrow perspective of their own environment, regarding them as something strange and incomprehensible. Consequently, they will never learn how to understand this other world and the powerful forces at work there. As long as they refuse to immerse yourself in the new and reflected business model, as long as they fail to discover what really makes it tick, they will never be able to reinvent their existing business model in a way that makes it sustainable in the changing digital world, where the customer is at the centre of everything. As long as they lack the courage to make the change and come to terms with the new and the strange, they will find themselves left behind in a world where their customers gradually disappear one by one, like figures from an Escher mirror, who escape from their own reflection and suddenly become real.

I realize that I am testing your resilience and perhaps even your credulity as my readers, but I am going to take things to yet another stage. If you refuse to embrace new models, so that you can understand them fully, and if you fail to learn and think in terms of reflected images, you will never be able to discover which of your own available business models is fitted for the New Normal world. Today's trendsetting companies have all adjusted their business model hundreds, if not thousands, of times through a process of trial and error. Sometimes, these changes are minor; sometimes, they are far-reaching. None of the world's great business giants operate today as they did when they first started. The basic outline of that first business plan is probably still recognizable, but none of their business models are set in stone. They are fluid, not rigid. In this way, the Apples and the Amazons are able to continue adding new insights to their progressive approach to doing business in a changing, upside down world.

Red ocean and blue ocean

I often find myself in meetings where start-ups make their pitches or nervous managers come to put forward their new ideas. You often hear the wise ladies and gentlemen of the adjudicating panel say something like: 'Is there really a blue ocean for your proposal?' A blue ocean... an undiscovered and untapped section of the market, as yet unclogged by the plastic waste of competition.

When we talk about innovation and start-ups, we are quick to assume that there is only something to be gained on condition that we can create an entirely new market. Why? Because the other markets are already covered by companies who are equally innovative, who 'excel in technology and their product-service combination'.

However, is this true? Do new companies always need to start in a completely new and open market? No, of course not. The idea that a start-up can only survive in a blue ocean is a fallacy. Look at the great disruptor companies of recent years. Most of them developed in a mature red ocean, in which established players fought tooth and nail to hold on to their share of the cake in a market where they believed the size of that cake was finite. A mistaken belief, as it turned out. Successful start-ups are able to find new (and often quite large) bits of cake, simply by looking in places and in ways that the 'big boys' are unwilling or unable to do. For example, by developing a business model that appeals to a customer segment that was previously disregarded.

Consider the following. If you want to take out a loan, you first need to meet certain criteria. These criteria are agreed by the banks amongst themselves, based on their many years of progressive insights. If you meet these criteria, their answer to your loan request will be positive; if you do not meet the criteria, it will be negative. Or at least that is the way it was until Avant came along. Avant is an American credit provider that uses data mining, machine learning and sophisticated algorithms to try and find potentially credit-worthy customers among those who have previously been refused loans by the traditional banks because they fail to meet the standard criteria. Avant was founded in 2012 and since then has generated revenues of 600 million dollars.[28] The company does not use digital technology to make its offers to prospective lenders quicker and more efficiently (although that is certainly one of the benefits), but rather to find ways to look beyond the restrictive limitations of the standard criteria. In other words, to develop a completely new business model, albeit one rooted in existing practices.

What if you are not able to develop a completely new market? Do you at least need a completely new product, something that dazzles with the brilliance of its new technology? Once again, I am going to have to disappoint you. Like the question 'Is there a blue ocean for your new product?', the question 'Is your product sufficiently radical?' is equally misplaced. Fossilized management still thinks that people can only be persuaded to buy or that markets can only be broken open with a revolutionary new concept. That is simply not true. It is not about new products and new technology. It is about more speed, comfort, simplicity, ease, access, freedom, etc. And, of course, a good price. If the perceived added value of the product on offer is worth the price, consumers will take the bait.

Starting a taxi company, a room leasing platform, a shoe company and a credit service: none of these things are likely to benefit from the luxury of a blue ocean. They are all products that already exist in one form or another. You can hardly call them radically new. Even so, disruptors like Uber, Airbnb, Amazon and Avant have succeeded in breaking the mould, not by developing their model in the old world, but as a mirror image in a kind of parallel dimension, with which they then break into the old world and take it by storm. Companies of this type are the answer to a frustrated consumer's prayers!

The disruptors do not even need to attack the established order head on. They simply offer the customer – who is looking for speed, comfort, simplicity, ease, access, freedom and a good price – their mirror model parallel to the existing model offered by others. They screen the market and carefully map consumer expectations, so they can target their offer accurately and expertly. They seek out the gaps in the existing market, in part thanks to a good dose of common sense, but also with the use of smart algorithms, thorough data analysis and perhaps even machine learning. The disruptors are able to thrive and prosper because of their progressive insight.

The 'old', existing players do almost the exact opposite. They forget to use their common sense, ignore the benefits of data analysis and smart algorithms, and simply carry on measuring all the things they have been measuring in the past, completely failing to recognize the changes in underlying consumer needs (and frustrations). As a result, they miss the boat – although they have no idea why.

The implementation of the disruptive and mirrored business model usually passes under the radar of the existing order, although it systematically eats away at their market. Sooner or later, they notice that their share of the cake is diminishing and respond by fighting in the only way they know: with the familiar weapons of their 'old' business model. They cannot understand what is happening – in fact, they deny that anything is happening for as long as possible – and fall back on the habits and instincts that are the norm in their world. They give their product a new colour, lobby the politicians to relax key legislation, make it harder for customers to defect, or start a price war. They try to lock down the market and continue their efforts to beat each other into submission. Which does not work.

The disruptors develop in the same ocean where so many other companies are bleeding to death, some faster than others. The disruptive model continues to attract increasing numbers of new customers, who in turn tell others about the product on offer, automatically adjusting their behaviour to the norms of the new universe, without even realizing it. Once you have been able to return three pairs of shoes free of charge, you expect to be able to do the same for every product. Once you have followed the approach of your taxi on your smartphone, you expect to be able to track all service providers. In this way, disruptors help to turn their ocean an even deeper shade of red. They have no need of a blue ocean to make the breakthrough with their clever idea. They are just as capable of turning a mature market upside down, putting the existing players under such pressure that they eventually eat each other up, one by one.

The car industry

The entire business model of the car industry is based on the principle of manufacturing as many cars as possible and selling them through dealerships. A number of other business models have been built around this basic model: the garage model, the second-hand car market model, the roadworks model, the petrol station model, the carwash model, the driving school model, etc. What is the purpose of a car? To drive us from point A to point B –and it is a purpose that has not changed during the past hundred years. Of course, the manner in which cars are nowadays developed and constructed is state of the art. Cars are increasingly safer, more comfortable, and more economical. Even so, the car remains essentially a private, fossil fuel-burning stove on wheels. What's more, your car is a closed system, which is completely self-contained. When you are not driving in your car, your investment is standing parked and unused – which is about 90% of the time. Every few thousand kilometres you take it to a garage to be serviced. And once it has reached a certain age or total mileage, you are tempted to replace it with a new one.

However, your new car is no longer a car – it is now a mobile computer. You no longer drive it from A to B; in the very near future it will be driving you instead. And when you are not using it, it will share its services to drive someone else from B to C. In short, it will lend itself to others. All the time it is on the road, your new car will be collecting data, which it will then pass on to other new cars, so that traffic in general becomes safer than it has ever been. And when your new car is standing still, it will now be standing at a battery charging point for electricity. As a result, it will require little or no mechanical maintenance – although you will still need to occasionally replace the tyres. All the rest is done automatically via software updates. As a result, your car has become a shared, open system.

In 2015, Mary Barra, the chairperson and CEO of GM, wrote the following to her shareholders: *'Across the industry and around the world, social and technological changes are transforming personal mobility. I believe the auto industry will change more in the next five years than it has in the last 50, as we develop new options and modes of transportation for moving us from point A to B.'*[29] The new car will transform the automobile industry root and branch. And not just the car industry, but also all the related satellite industries that orbit in the car universe. The car will become mobility and mobility will be an app. In the future, car dealers will not sell a hundred cars to a hundred different people, but just a few cars whose use will be shared by those same hundred people. Less maintenance means fewer garages. Fewer accidents mean less insurance. The likelihood that my grandson will need a driving license when he grows up is non-existent. The classic fossil fuel-burning stove on wheels will go the same way as the horse: it will either be used in poorer countries or it will become a nostalgic weekend toy for the rich and famous. If you work in the petrol or diesel industry, your business model is being wiped out right in front of your very eyes. Much the same is true for public transport, since the new car will make our private transport available to everyone!

Why will this new mobility take the world by storm? Because autonomous electrical technology has created a shift in consumer demand. People are no longer willing to accept that cars pollute our environment. They like the idea of being able to relax or work during the journey from A to B. Above all, they like the idea that the self-driving, shared car will save them time, money and a whole heap of misery.

Mary Barra of GM is one of the key figures in the car industry who understood this. The huge German car giants are not far behind. A few years ago, they laughed at the wild plans of Elon Musk; now they are doing their best to try and catch him up. But it isn't easy for them. Classic car manufacturers find it hard to escape their traditional linear way of thinking. Most of them are still locked into the 'start-hold-repeat' mode, but whereas in the past they used to set the tone, now they are forced to follow the lead of others. Even a brand like Porsche is working on a Tesla-killer: the Mission E. Or that, at least, is what the press is reporting.[30] What intrigues me about this is not so much the idea of an electric Porsche, but rather what the use of words like 'Tesla-killer' and 'Mission' say about the emotions that are being stirred up in Sindelfingen, the town where the majority of Porsches are made. For the very first time, car manufacturers are being confronted with changes that they do not control and which, even worse, threaten to undermine their business model (and their technology, in which they have invested billions over the years).

Even so, it is noticeable that the majority of classic manufactures persist in thinking in terms of '*das Auto*'. They build an electric car simply to replace a petrol-driven one. They develop technology to allow for the shared used of transport not from a holistic vision about mobility, but to show that their technological skills are still up to speed and that they can play the Tesla game as well as anybody else. What they are, in fact, doing is attempting to stretch the life of their existing model, rather than turning it upside down. Even if they succeed, their success is likely to be short-lived. At some point soon, the politicians are certain to intervene and say: 'Fossil fuel cars can ride until such-and-such a date and no further.' And 'such-and-such a date' probably means until 2030 or 2035.

The car industry still lacks the courage to see that the change is about much more than the installation of an electric motor instead of a petrol one or the creation of a car that recognizes you and allows you to choose your own preferred colour for its interior lighting. The change is about the application of a completely new business model that mirrors the existing one, but implements it in a completely different way.

The future of the motor car is ACES. This acronym stands for Autonomous, Connected, Electric and Shared. You can already see the signals of this future wherever you look. Uber, Lyft and Waymo already have self-driving vehicles on the road. The number of hybrid and electric cars is on the rise. In contrast, diesel is on the way out – for good. Every major car brand is working on an ACES variant. Look at GM and Ford, who have set a date for the mass production of autonomous cars without a steering wheel and pedals at 2019 and 2021 respectively. And every modern city has its own policies and initiatives relating to car sharing. In the meantime, the traffic on our roads keeps on getting busier and busier, to the frustration of drivers around the world. In the near future, all these forces will combine to create an entirely new car business based on an entirely new mobility model, which will change patterns of consumer expectation almost overnight.

The old car brands fail to realize that these forces are already on the way; that a new reality is already being created on the other side of the mirror; and that more and more customers are willing to embrace this new reality. In contrast, Tesla has been working for some time with the new business and mobility models, and is helping to change consumer behaviour as a result. Each time the classic brands announce the launch of a Tesla-killer, which they expect to have in production by 2022 or later, I am struck by just how limited their thinking really is. They continue to fight Tesla with the weapons of their old world, the world of 'the best car or nothing', of driving pleasure and technological gimmickry. They are still living in the surface world, where the focus is on the biggest number of cars, the biggest number of models and the greatest number of sales, with customers buying a new variant every four, five or six years. They believe that Tesla also lives in this world and that consequently they will be able to crush Elon Musk and his dreams. 'Just a little bit longer,' they think, 'and then we will have him'. But Tesla does not live in their world. Tesla lives in the upside down underworld. Tesla breaks conventions. Tesla changes consumer behaviour. Tesla rewrites the rules of the game. In short, Tesla creates a mirror-image model for the car industry of the future.

The TREE principle

The shift that is taking place in the car and mobility market is a perfect example of the TREE principle:

1) *Technology* first: the technology undergoes an exponential evolution. The car of the future is a robot, directed by AI and big data, which will also revolutionize all related business models in the same manner.
2) *Red ocean:* the market is a red ocean, in which existing customers are frustrated. Private car ownership is expensive and polluting. For 90% of the time your car is parked somewhere; for the other 10% you are probably sitting in a traffic jam. Cars damage the environment and 'cost' human lives, both in terms of accidents and pollution-related disease.
3) *Engagement* with the customer: the consumer who opts for this different kind of mobility will never want to go back to the old ways and will be happy to inspire other consumers to do the same.

4) *Ecosystem:* universities, start-ups and technology players work separately and together on the ACES aspects. They stimulate each other to make new discoveries and attract huge amounts of investment capital.

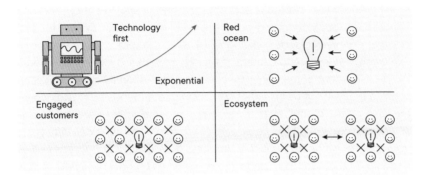

The TREE principle for exponential growth

If a market meets the criteria of the TREE principle, you can expect exponential disruption to follow soon. The problem with the old car industry is that it is not yet willing or able to make the necessary quantum leap, because the leading manufacturers have waited too long before attempting to develop a viable alternative. As a result, they are still not ready to take the next (admittedly major) step towards a new business model. On the one hand, their thinking is governed by the idea that the new model will still take quite some time to arrive, so that they prefer to carry on milking the existing model for as long as they can. On the other hand, they do not actually have a plan B to offer, even if they do suddenly see the need to ditch the old model. Consequently, the continued milking of their outdated plan A remains the only option.

My neighbour also milks cows. And his cows are fitted with pedometers or step counters. The information from the step counters has allowed him to learn that if a cow suddenly begins to take a lot of steps, exactly sixteen hours later is the best moment to let that cow be artificially inseminated. He no longer needs the services of a vet to pick the right moment. The same data model also tells him that a time span of less that sixteen hours increases the likelihood of a female calf, while a time span of more than sixteen hours increases the likelihood of a male calf. Nowadays, everything can be connected. And everything that is connected can be read and activated. The connection itself is not so important. What is important is what you do with all those connected elements and what you are able to achieve with them for each person as an individual and for society as a whole.

In a cloud of laughing gas

If your programme has a good title, why change it? That is probably what the people at the BBC think. *Horizon* is that kind of programme. It has been running under the same title for more than 50 years. Two thousand one hundred episodes of cutting-edge scientific investigation. One of the first black-and-white episodes, dating from 1964, explored 'The Knowledge Explosion'.[31] In a piece to camera, sci-fi legend Arthur C. Clarke talks about the development of the transistor and the geo-stationary communication satellite that will put us in instant contact with our friends no matter where they live on the planet, even if we do not know exactly where they are at any given moment: *'It will be possible in that age, perhaps only fifty years from now, for a man to conduct his business from Tahiti or Bali, just as well as he could from London. I am perfectly serious when I suggest one day we may have surgeons in Edinburgh operating on patients in New Zealand.'*

Arthur C. Clarke was also responsible, together with Stanley Kubrick, for writing the scenario for one of the most iconic and visionary science fiction films of all time: *2001: A Space Odyssey*. This film released in 1968, but four years earlier (probably in September 1964 according to YouTube, where you can watch the fragment) he was less sanguine about people's response to such a vision: *'Trying to predict the future is a discouraging and hazardous occupation, because the prophet invariably falls between two stools. If his prediction sounds at all reasonable, you can be quite sure that in 20 or at most 50 years, the progress of science and technology has made him seem ridiculously conservative. On the other hand, if by some miracle a prophet exactly describes the future as it was going to take place, his prediction would seem so absurd, so farfetched, that everybody would laugh him to scorn. This is proven to be true in the past, and it will undoubtedly be true even more so in the century to come.'*

On 9 January 2007, Steve Jobs unveiled the first iPhone with the words: *'Well, today, we are introducing three revolutionary products of this class. The first one is a widescreen iPod with touch controls. The second is a revolutionary mobile phone. And the third is a breakthrough Internet communications device.'*[32] This speech by Jobs is compulsory viewing for every manager and can be viewed in its entirety on YouTube. It is also worth checking out a second YouTube film made just a few days later. Steve Ballmer, who was then the CEO at Microsoft, is sitting in a film studio. A journalist asks Ballmer what he thought when Jobs pulled his new toy out of his magician's hat. Ballmer replied condescendingly: *'500 dollars? Fully subsidized, with a plan? I would say that is the most expensive phone in the world! And it does not appeal to business customers, because it does not have a keyboard, which makes it not a very good e-mail machine. Now, it may sell very well or not, you know. But we have our strategy; we've got great Windows mobile devices in the market today. You can get a Motorola Q phone now for 99 dollars. It's a very capable machine. It'll do music, it'll do internet. It'll do email, it'll do instant messaging. I kind of looked at that and I said, well, I like our strategy, I like it a lot.'*

New things are often laughed out of court on the basis judgements made using an old frame of reference. There is a German word for this: *hincin-Interpretieren*. It means something like 'reinterpretation' – but a reinterpretation based on prejudice. The new innovation will 'obviously' not be successful, because traditional KPIs place the emphasis elsewhere. This is what Steve Ballmer was doing in that TV interview: interpreting the iPhone from his own frame of reference and subjecting it to existing KPI norms: a good phone and texting machine that also offers internet and music, but oh so expensive! This analysis is hardly surprising: Microsoft's KPIs were designed to justify and extend the life of their own business model.

Outdated KPIs are ideal for rationalizing the fear of the new. Laughing at smart but unfamiliar ideas is one of the best ways to kill off innovation. People use laughter as an antidote to stress and anxiety. So do not get taken in by the laughter of others. If people in your company start laughing at new competitors, that is the time to start ringing the alarm bell. In 2016, Ballmer admitted that it was a big mistake not moving into the handheld device business earlier. Above all, he wished he had cottoned on to the way Apple planned to make their business model work, through the subsidies of mobile providers: '*I wish I would have thought about the model of subsidizing phones through the operators,*' he told Bloomberg.[33]

'IF PEOPLE IN YOUR COMPANY STARTING LAUGHING AT NEW COMPETITORS, IT IS TIME TO START RINGING THE ALARM BELL.'

Ballmer should have known better. His own boss, Bill Gates, had been on the receiving end of the same kind of prejudice. When Bill Gates provided 'Big Blue' IBM with the DOS operating systems for PCs – for a ridiculous one-off fee of 80,000 dollars – he was smart enough to hold on to the copyright.[34] Why? Because he was convinced that 'soon everyone will have a PC in their home'. Of course, no-one believed him. At the time, the captains of industry could not envisage such a thing. A PC in every home? What on earth would people do with them? But Gates could see what the captains could not – and the rest, as they say, is history. MS-DOS conquered the world and today we are knee-deep in personal computers.

Jack Welch, who was head of the giant General Electric for more than 20 years, once said: *'If the rate of change on the outside exceeds the rate of change on the inside, the end is near.'* I fear that many companies are blind to the turning point for their own particular cash-cow when it comes. They fail to pick up the signals that herald its arrival and are dazzled by the success of their old model. After all, that model has served them well for many years, has it not? So why should they start doubting it now? Conviction becomes faith –and so they carry on doing 'what we are good at'.

Another potential pitfall is the familiarity of the old frames of reference and the rules that govern their operation. Because we have mastered the use of this framework and these rules so well over so many years, and because we have built up so many structures, methods and processes around them, we want to hang on to them for as long as we possibly can. After all, we have invested a small fortune in them. Not just money, but also time and energy. What are we supposed to do? Just throw all this out of the window? What is more, the old, familiar systems confer a certain status on 'the powers that be'. A new way of thinking means new structures, methods and processes. And perhaps also new kids on the block. Change always demands major effort and is never without risk.

There is misleading laughter. There is blindness. There is lazy thinking. However, this does not explain everything that can (and frequently does) go wrong. Companies can also fall from their pedestal because they no longer possess the instruments they need to translate the necessary change into practice within their own organizational set-up. Or perhaps the key elements of the message get lost in translation. Or maybe they are doing 95% of things right, but the key to success lies in the missing 5%? Picking up the pass, dribbling the entire defence, dummying the goalkeeper... and then blasting the ball over the bar of the open goal: it even happens to the best footballers.

The smartphone was not invented by Apple. Nokia had the Communicator. And BlackBerry had the BlackBerry. These first smartphones were intended for people who wanted to send e-mails on the move. And who were the people who wanted that in the 1990s and in the first decade of the new century? Managers. And only managers. The keyboard was perfect for this purpose. And only for this purpose. The Nokia Communicator was built like a brick (and almost as heavy), but it was a great device in its own way.

For several years, the BlackBerry was a 'must-have' for ambitious high-potentials. Both phones did exactly what managers wanted. Nothing more, nothing less. There was no music. No camera. No colours...

Nokia and BlackBerry were wiped out a number of years ago. Did both companies make a mistake? No, it is simply that Steve Jobs and Jonathan Ivy at Apple did the same thing better – and in a different way. Their design and touchscreen invested the smartphone with emotion. Instead of being a 'must-have' for managers, it became a 'must-have' for everyone. They transformed the early warning signals first activated by Nokia and BlackBerry into a shark's fin, colouring the ocean an even deeper shade of red...

The adaptive cycle

Today, the traditional giants, business gurus and even start-up pioneers are all saying more or less the same. Even though we hardly realize it, all the rules of the game have changed. The world has been turned upside down. In fact, the rules have been changed so thoroughly that it is not even the same game anymore. We need to play in a completely different way.

If an environment starts to invert and its paradigm starts to lose its dominance, companies are often faced with a variety of dilemmas. Is it better to be a trendsetter or a trend-follower? Should we install the new ground-breaking software immediately or should we wait a while? What should we keep and what should we scrap? The greater the uncertainty, unpredictability and confusion in the environment, the greater the number of such dilemmas becomes. Toon Abcouwer at the University of Amster-

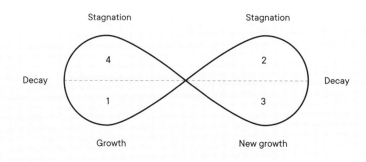

The adaptive cycle of resilience model. Growth is never endless.

dam has developed a model that shows how companies can react in a dynamic environment when things begin to shift. His 'adaptive cycle of resilience' model assumes that every company undergoes a cyclical path of development. This path is divided over four quadrants. The development is determined on the one hand by what the company wants and on the other hand by what it can do. Throughout the company's life there will also be periods of both certainty and uncertainty. These variables are different for each company.

A company typically starts in an environment where it knows with certainty what it wants and what it can do. There is balance. The company produces, the customers are satisfied and there is no reason to make new choices. Quadrant 1 is the quadrant of 'business as usual'. I describe this as dynamic expansion. Everything is going well for the company.

Look at the world of banking. The business model of our major banks is essentially the same as the model developed during the early Renaissance by the bankers in 14th century Tuscany, Venice and Genoa. Banks lend money at a rate of interest and trade in currencies. For hundreds of years, the banks have been able to integrate changes in the world into this classic Renaissance model with relative ease.

The danger of this 'relaxed' situation is that it increases the risk of losing sight of future developments, both internal and external, and of ignoring the advent of new and groundbreaking technology. When this happens, the organization is often late to initiate the changes it needs to meet the new situation. There is now an imbalance and the company evolves towards quadrant 2.[35] Uncertainty begins to raise its ugly head. Have we still got what it takes to succeed? The future becomes uncertain. At this point, a great deal depends on the management and inspirational skills of the organization's leader. This is when you need someone like Jamie Dimon of J.P. Morgan, who realized that the banking model had reached a turning point and had the courage to say: *'We can no longer rely on our old methods of integration and assimilation: we need to reinvent ourselves.'* Because it is difficult to grasp and understand new evolutions, the focus is often placed on the development of new skills and increased flexibility. Possibilities are explored, external knowledge is brought in, partnerships are formed. As these processes start to bear fruit, so the company evolves toward quadrant 3.[36]

Quadrant 3 is the 'action' quadrant. Research and development is prioritized. Pilots are tested. Scenario analyses are conducted. The organization builds up a range of options from which it can later choose. This is a critical phase, because the key to renewed success depends on making the right (and hopefully best) choice. But be careful: this is also the moment when the internal politics of the organization are at their most volatile. Playing power games at the wrong moment can jeopardize everything.

Once the company has made its choice, it will move towards quadrant 4. This essentially involves upscaling and improving the new product. This requires the development of new processes, the making of new arrangements and the streamlining of everything the company does. Quadrant 4 is the quadrant of far-reaching change. It is only now that you will see whether or not the choice you made was the right one. If you picked a winner, your company will be re-launched and will return to a position of 'business as usual', with a relative state of balance between what it wants and what it can do.[37] If you picked a loser, your company is probably dead and buried. The 'adaptive cycle of resilience' model posits that as long as everything remains in balance, a 'problem' can be solved using the classic instruments. But if, at a given moment, your company's world is turned upside down, this classic repertoire will no longer be enough to save you. This is when you need to follow new paths. Curiosity plays a crucial role. The company must turn its back on the status quo, dare to think intuitively and search for what Abcouwer describes as 'relative revolt'. Unless you can achieve this state of revolt, you will find yourself getting deeper and deeper in trouble. Be aware, however, that the revolt is supposed to be 'relative': you don't need to jettison everything from the past. Instead, you should build on the good elements,[38] holding on to the aspects of your organizational DNA that are worth keeping. Abcouwer refers to this as the 'remember' influence. Once again, balance is key: too much 'remember' leads to rigidity.

It is perhaps no coincidence that Abcouwer and Goesen chose the infinity symbol to visualize their model. In the 'adaptive cycle of resilience', companies are in continuous movement from one quadrant to another. In today's world, however, it is vital to take action to sharpen your skills and to use your inspirational abilities as a leader before the crisis arrives. It is wise to assume that everything is more or less in a state of permanent semi-imbalance. It is almost as if you need to be active in all four quadrants at the same time. Not to continually change everything, but to develop a range of options for choice. Not to panic, but to remain agile and resilient.

If you are still thinking in the 'business as usual' mode, this means that you have failed to notice the imbalances in your situation. If you wait until the crisis explodes in your face before developing new pilots and making new choices, you will be hopelessly too late. Nowadays, speed is the most important competitive advantage. It is no longer the big companies who beat the little ones. It is the fast companies who beat the slow ones. Constantly questioning what you do and considering new options must be an automatic part of your company health check. Focus your gaze both inwards and outwards. Don't simply look at today, but also at tomorrow and the day after tomorrow. Based on your vision of the future, do all that you can now to shape your future within that vision. Set the bar high. Dare to think and act boldly: aim for the stars, in order to hit the moon. From now on, you need to think in terms of 'whatever it takes'.

The exponential curve

Exponential technology thinkers like to model their thinking on Moore's Law. Gordon Moore was one of the founders of chip producer Intel. In the *Electronics* magazine of 19 April 1965, he predicted that technological progress would make it possible for the number of transistors on a microchip to double each year.[39] Later, he amended this prediction to a doubling every two years.

Moore's Law has been a good indicator of the technological leaps and bounds the world has made during the past half century – and will continue to make. We are currently at the computing equivalent of a mouse's brain and we will soon be rising rapidly to the equivalent of a human brain. What is more (no pun intended), it is no longer simply a matter of computing power; today's microchips have a variety of different functions built into them: image sensors, fluid sensors, antennas, batteries, etc. The quantity of data also continues to increase exponentially, in part because the number of devices generating data is likewise increasing exponentially, as are the possibilities for making, combining and storing that data. It is expected that by 2020 we will all create a combined world total of 44 zettabytes of digital data each year. This is likely to rise to an astronomical 167 zettabytes by 2025.[40] That is ten times the quantity in 2016. To give you some idea of just how much this is, one zettabyte is equivalent to a trillion gigabytes or 1,000,000,000,000,000,000,000 (10^{21}) bytes.

'CONSTANTLY QUESTIONING WHAT YOU DO AND CONSIDERING NEW OPTIONS MUST BE AN AUTOMATIC PART OF YOUR COMPANY HEALTH CHECK.'

It is important to realize that this huge and exponential technological growth is the result of a succession of technologies, which have mutually complemented, strengthened and in some cases even replaced each other. This is logical: the impact of a single technology can never continue to grow exponentially ad infinitum. Each individual technology experiences periods of expansion, maturity and decline. A point is eventually reached when the technology passes its high-water mark and is confronted with the limit of its possibilities. The margin for further growth shrinks. This is when a new technology is needed to revitalize or replace the old one. First there was the radio valve, then the transistor, then the microchip... And in the future?

At the end of 2006, Moore said that his law would not remain eternally valid. There are physical limitations that cannot be exceeded. For a transistor, this limit is equivalent to a dozen or so atoms: it is impossible to make a transistor any smaller. This still leaves a lot of theoretical room for further improvement, but in practice we are still a long way off from the technology that will make atom-size production processes a reality. Consequently, we still need to develop new technologies that will bring us closer and closer to these physical boundaries, like the neuromorphic chip of IMEC, a chip that learns through experience and continually adjusts its architecture,[41] in much the same way that our human brain makes and breaks connections in response to new input.

You can also see the limits of exponential technological growth in your own home. You can only operate as many touchscreens as you have hands and fingers. You can only have as many data-collecting, inter-communicating Home Pods, thermostats, refrigerators, vacuum cleaners and other household devices as your house can hold. Unless, of course, a completely different kind of technology unexpectedly arrives on the scene or a brand new type of information suddenly becomes important.

S-curves

In his book *The New Normal*, technology entrepreneur Peter Hinssen describes the life cycle of technology as an S-curve.[42] Each successful technology follows a line of progression shaped like a letter 'S'.

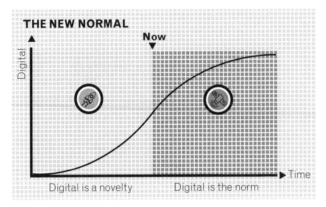

Exponential growth levels out toward the end.

At the start, a new technology typically experiences teething problems and is generally less efficient than existing technologies. There is also a degree of resistance: 'new' means different. Once these initial problems have been solved and people become more familiar with the newness of the technology, the search can begin to find its best possible applications. If these applications have an eager market, the technology can have an exponential impact and 'change the world'. But the increase in this impact will inevitably tail off at some point, because the technology has reached the limit of its possibilities.

Once this 'ageing' technology has passed the pinnacle of its popularity, there is a real risk of decline setting in, perhaps because a newer, better technology has now appeared on the market. When this happens, the 'old' technology is quickly superseded: it has become obsolete and is no longer desirable. This is the situation where typically the owners of the technology try to milk their 'cow' for as long as possible. They reject the idea of innovation and renewal until it is absolutely necessary. They only think about breeding or buying a new cow when the existing one has been milked dry.

Today's disruptors pose a serious challenge to this scenario. They do not think in terms of technology per se, but in terms of combinations and applications that can work to the benefit of the customer. They take no account of the customs of a sector or 'normal business'. They do not even wait until the existing technology or business model has reached maturity before launching a new variant. They take bold action at a much earlier stage and you do not need to be a genius to guess the likely effect: the established order is taken completely by surprise.

In other words, the purveyors of disruptive business models aimed at new technologies effectively build new S-curves on top of existing ones – and they do it more quickly than is classically expected. Over time, this leads to a rapid accumulation of S-curves, one on top of the other, with knock-on effects for all the technology providers and their related business models. This accumulation of S-curves creates an exponentially growing 'technological cloud' of possibilities for the customer.

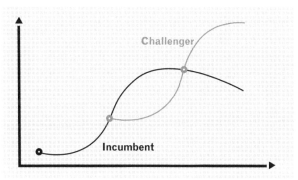

Source: Chris Bradley and Clayton O'Toole,
An Incumbent's Guide to Digital Disruption, McKinsey Quarterly, May 2016

The original S-curve is replaced by the following S-curve before its exponential growth tails off.

There is more to it than Moore

The winners in the new upside down world seem as though they are able to free themselves from all the restrictions of the old world. It is a bit like setting a new world record for the high jump, but instead of improving the figures from 2.45 metres to say 2.47 metres immediately clearing a height of 12.30 metres!

Tech-nerds delight in trying to find ways to explain the exponential changes in the world through technological evolutions. I often find their explanations too strongly focused on technology alone or too much interpreted from a purely technological perspective. For me, their theories are never complete and never completely satisfactory. I can certainly follow them to some extent, but their ideas fail to properly explain all the changes we have seen in recent times. There are other forces at work under the tech-radar. And all these force have an impact on each other.

You can view these recent developments as a roller-coaster ride, where each car sets in motion the next one in the chain. If you look at the current wave of disruption from this perspective, you can see that there is not just a single (technological) acceleration, but that technology has helped to generate five further disruptive accelerations. Seen in these terms, Moore's Law is for wimps. Every flywheel that is kick-started in the new world activates in turn a further acceleration in an even higher gear. This fivefold acceleration is the unique feature of our age. It is companies like Google, Facebook, Alibaba, Tencent and Amazon who are now leading the new dance.

'MOORE'S LAW IS FOR WIMPS. EVERY FLYWHEEL THAT IS KICK-STARTED IN THE NEW WORLD ACTIVATES IN TURN A FURTHER ACCELERATION IN AN EVEN HIGHER GEAR.'

1) The first acceleration is based on a technological evolution, which makes more things possible at an exponential rate. Companies try to exploit these possibilities to the best of their ability. This is Moore's Law.

2) The second acceleration is based on fields of tension in existing markets. Companies in the digital underworld develop mirror-image models for markets where there are lots of customers wrestling with various forms of dissatisfaction (stress, lack of user-friendliness, etc.). These disruptors persuade customers to switch to their alternative model. The greater the level of tension imposed by the old models on their customers, the greater the surge of reactive energy when a new alternative appears, resulting in an exponential increase in the number of people defecting from the old model to the new.

3) The third acceleration is based on the power of social networks, both online and offline. The first customer makes two new customers. These two new customers in turn make four other new customers. Four becomes eight. Eight becomes sixteen, and so on. The energy to share in this way is present in abundance. In this respect, people have not changed. What has changed is their interactions and their behaviour. In our hyper-connected world customers drag other customers along with them and together they form an exponentially growing sales and marketing department.

4) The fourth acceleration is based on an increasing demand for more new technology. It is the technology-driven companies that are best able to persuade customers to change their behaviour. When this happens, it always results in the customers setting the new bar even higher, so that there are plenty of opportunities for further technological innovation. Once they have experienced the benefits of technology in one field, they want to experience it in other fields as well. In other words, there is a significant margin for further growth (the process has only just begun). Consequently, changing customer behaviour strengthens the demand for more new technology and its exponential application in wider fields. The chicken becomes the egg.

5) What about the fifth acceleration? The new companies, which develop exponentially in the new world, can soon think about sailing beyond their red ocean and into adjoining ones, which they can then add to their ever expanding cathedral (Facebook), city (Amazon or Alibaba), country (Google) or universe (Tencent). In the new world, new ecosystems develop that mutually and exponentially strengthen each other.

Exponential is not manageable

Organizations are under a great deal of pressure. If you failed to see the shark's fin in the distance, if you waited too long to respond or exhausted yourself by trying to put up barriers to its approach, you risk finding yourself overwhelmed when your market suddenly turns turtle.

The trick is to prepare and launch your new business model while the existing one is still popular with customers. This is easier said than done, of course. Giving up on an existing business model that is still booking good results is by no means straightforward. Why should you exchange the certainty of something that works for the uncertainty of something that has yet to prove its value? Such a decision is highly counter-intuitive. And so you put out more deckchairs on the beach. True, you put them a little closer together than in the past, but what is the problem with that: there is still plenty of room. Okay, perhaps you can see a tsunami gathering on the horizon, but it is still a long way off and from here on your beach the wave looks pretty small. However, standing on the beach, it is impossible to judge with what speed it is racing towards you. By the time you finally realize the true magnitude of the onrushing wall of water, it is already too late.

This is the great challenge: having the courage to continually re-write your business model, gradually adjusting, improving and retesting it, so that when the right wave comes along you can actually ride it rather than being engulfed by it. Of course, this means taking risks. It also means you cannot be afraid of waves and have to accept that you might occasionally suffer a wipe-out. However, if you succeed, you will be faster than all the others and can upscale your activities like never before.

Essentially, this comes down to always thinking ahead and always asking yourself if you can improve on what you are already doing for your customers. You need to be constantly on your guard, constantly ready to act. You cannot wait to follow the lead of others. You need to be ahead of the game, so that others must try to follow you – if they can.

Disruptors think out of the box and supplement their business model almost non-stop, after the necessary testing. When they see a wave coming, they set out more sail rather than pulling sail down, so that they can ride the wave harder and faster. Disruptors never complain when they see a wave approaching. On the contrary, it is what they have been waiting for. So try to be like them.

Even so, a word of warning is necessary. Demonstrating courage and foresight is good as long as you do not take things too far. There is a risk that exponential thinking will take over the change processes in your company, until they become like a kind of dogma. In fact, you often hear it said at congresses and seminars: 'If you want to keep up to speed as a company, you have to change exponentially'.

Is this true? The world might be changing exponentially, but does your company have to do the same? Well, no. In fact, in my opinion it is a myth to believe that companies are capable of changing exponentially. To say that a company must change exponentially is the same as saying that there must be constant change, all the time. That is fine and might even be fun for a small start-up, but in larger companies non-stop change only leads to chaos. And chaos solves nothing. Quite the opposite.

Evolution is a constant in any environment, but that does not mean that you need to continually overturn or move the basic building blocks of your company. If you do so, your entire organizational structure will come tumbling down. Non-stop change weakens the foundations that ensure the stability of your company. Besides, constant technological change is a massively expensive business. Very few companies can afford to make this change on an almost daily basis.

What you need is the right dynamic balance between preservation and renewal, between development and production. If a process works well, that is great! Make sure you keep it and do not ditch it unnecessarily.

Like companies, it is also impossible for human beings to change exponentially. Our brains just keep getting in the way. Human behaviour does not evolve exponentially in the same manner as technology, but evolves discontinuously, in leaps and bounds. People only summon up the courage to change if they can see the point and feel safe with it. Even then, it takes time before they come to terms with it and accept it fully. What's more, different people take the step toward change at different times: there are early adopters, followers, laggards and critics. And since companies are made by people, company evolution also takes place in a succession of leaps and bounds.

'HUMAN BEHAVIOUR DOES NOT EVOLVE EXPONENTIALLY, BUT DISCONTINUOUSLY, IN LEAPS AND BOUNDS.'

The key to success lies in knowing what works and what does not. You need to critically examine your traditions on a regular basis. What can you already change today in order to survive and thrive tomorrow and the day after tomorrow? However, do not forget that change for change's sake is always counter-productive. You cannot force people to change. That never works. Change is only productive if you know precisely why you want to change. If you can explain this convincingly to your people and persuade them to share your vision of what the change is supposed to achieve, only then will they be willing to follow.

Close the gap

The following illustrations show the different kinds of developmental path over time.

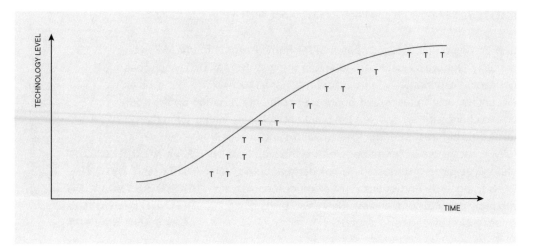

Technology Frontier over time.

First, there is the technological cloud, the collection of technology that at any moment in time represents the state of the art. Technologies follow each other in rapid succession, increasing in number and complexity, expanding in scope exponentially. The cloud contains a staggeringly wide range of technical options, from the most extreme to the most accessible, each offering myriad connections and leads. The technological cloud leaves an exponential track through time, in which you can plot a steeply climbing and undulating line, like an upper limit to the possibilities a form of technology has to offer.

The second cloud is the cloud of customer expectations. As customers, we embrace the technology and the resultant basic models if they fulfil a need or provide a better solution than currently exists in the market. At any moment in time there are customers who live comfortably in the technological cloud, keen to immediately adopt the most recent innovations (early adopters). Other customers react more slowly (the followers), while at the other end of the spectrum there are customers who are reluctant to accept the new technology (laggards and critics). That being said, once people actually take the step towards a new technology, they usually absorb it quickly.

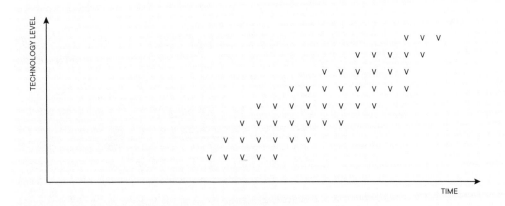

Cloud of customer expectations over time

At any moment in time, there are collections of customers whose expectations are either closer to or further away from the exponential technology curve. If, as a customer, you enjoy a positive experience, you expect to have that same experience from other providers. As a result, customer expectations tend to quickly follow whatever is technologically possible. Over time, the level of expectation increases, also among the followers, because the early adopters have told them about their positive experiences, so that the followers now want to try out the new technology for

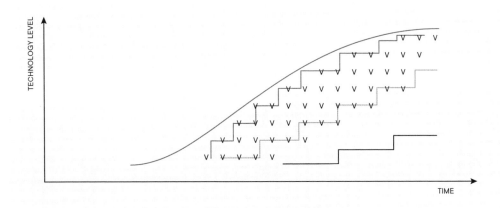

Red: Technology Frontier
Blue: Evolution of client expectations as early adopter over time
Grey: Evolution of client expectations as slow adopter over time
Black: Evolution of client expectations as outsider

themselves. And once they are convinced of its benefits (easier, friendlier, simpler, faster, liberating, more respectful, etc.), they want this kind of technology everywhere. What was non-existent or outrageously luxurious yesterday is normal today. By tomorrow it will be a minimum and by the day after tomorrow it will be obsolete.

The third curve (bottom of the previous page) shows the value proposition of a company that is good at what it does, but does not innovate in depth. It is reluctant to introduce new technology until absolutely necessary. The company continues to work with its existing tools in its existing manner. For them, innovation means that a product might occasionally be given a new colour or new packaging. If the value proposition does not alter (remains constant over time), you will get a completely horizontal value curve. If occasional incremental innovation is implemented, the value curve will be transformed into a series of small steps. The value proposition certainly increases, but it is unlikely to hit the headlines in the trade press.

I am not arguing that a constant value proposition is a bad thing. It depends on your customer group. If you are a manufacturer of cuckoo clocks, you make your living from tradition and your tradition-loving customers are prepared to pay for that tradition. But even a cuckoo clock company can benefit from having an online forum and shop. And who knows: with a 3D-printed clock you might be able to appeal to a brand-new target audience. Perhaps the real cuckoo fanatics might even be willing to design their own clocks and share these with others.

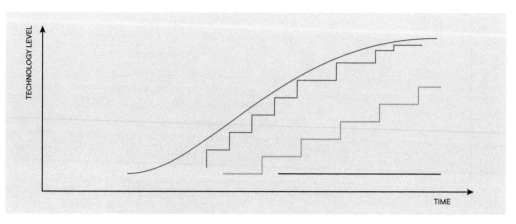

Red: Technology Frontier
Blue: Value proposition innovator following technology from up close
Grey: Value proposition sporadic incremental innovation
Black: Constant value proposition over time

Companies that pay no attention to technological evolution and to changes in customer expectation follow a development path that takes them further and further away from the ideal path (technological cloud, customer cloud). By adopting a persistently rigid approach and failing to take fundamental steps to renew their business model, such companies are eventually pushed towards the margin. And the margin is a place where companies go to die.

The fourth stepped 'curve' (bottom of the previous page) shows the value proposition of a company that follows the needs and wants of its customers and attempts to provide customer satisfaction by surfing on the right technological wave. At regular intervals, the company is prepared to radically revise its business model or to launch new products. The introduction of new technology, the development of an improved value proposition for the customer, and the subsequent adjustment of the business model all take time and careful preparation. The evolution of the value proposition therefore takes place in fits and starts.

The faster the iterations, the more agile and flexible the company, the more frequent the periods of renewal, the less dramatic they need to be and the closer the company can match its value proposition to the expectations of its customers. The separate sections of straight lines can either run horizontally or be inclined, depending on whether the offer remains 'frozen' or whether it gradually reflects customer expectation, without the need for major innovative efforts in new technology.

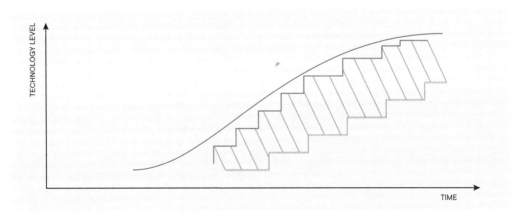

Red: Technology Frontier
Blue: Evolution of customer expectations Y over time
Grey: Value proposition of brand X over time
Green: market tension between customer expectation and market offer, space for disruption

'YOUR OWN SENSE OF DISRUPTION SHOULD TELL YOU HOW FAR YOUR OWN EVOLUTION IS LAGGING BEHIND THE EVOLUTIONS TAKING PLACE BEYOND YOUR OWN IMMEDIATE ENVIRONMENT.'

The space between the exponential curves of the technology offered and customer expectation on the one hand and the company's value proposition on the other, is the space where disruption is possible. The greater the gap between customer expectation and the market offer, the greater the field of market tension and the easier for a disruptor to wipe out your business overnight. Disruption is the gap between the speed with which the worlds of technology, markets and customer expectation evolve on the one hand and the speed with which companies change to reflect and exploit these factors on the other hand. Your own sense of disruption should tell you how far your own evolution is lagging behind the evolutions taking place beyond your own immediate environment.

Exit the word 'disruption'

Disruption is possible at any moment, and usually there is no warning in advance. At least, not according to those who are disrupted.

Typically, companies react in one of the following ways (or a combination thereof) to the arrival of a disruptor in their market.

1) They keep on milking the cow currently in the stable. They have great faith in their own technology and business model. The technology is still gaining in maturity and the point of decline has not yet been reached. To begin with, the impact of the new disruptor business model will be relatively small. It will nibble away at their share of the market, but the damage is slight and the situation in general is still favourable. And so they carry on as normal. There is still plenty of time to react should things take a turn for the worse.

2) They interpret the signals within the existing framework. For a long time they have noticed nothing and now are suddenly confronted with change. This demands a quick reaction – but it is usually the wrong one. The signals are now being picked up – loud and clear – but they are interpreted (remember our word *hineininterpretiert*?) within the current context of the market. The result is neither one thing nor the other. They make efforts to respond but they fail to address the real problem. A waste of time, in fact. It will not help to put your washing powder in Apple packaging!

3) They react with a misplaced confidence: 'This might affect others but it will not affect us'. Many companies regard their position as impregnable. They see the signals of change, but fail to link them to possible consequences for themselves. Overestimating oneself is a human weakness – and often found in the biggest and the best. They are certain that their size, history and past success will keep them safe.

4) They put all their energy into defence. They organize extra advertising for their own product, they pour negative publicity on the weak points of the disruptive offer and they do everything possible to keep the disruptor at an arm's length by erecting barriers in the form of lobby work and new regulations.

5) They reinvent themselves and pick a new wave. They start with a clean sheet marked with three columns: Discard – Keep – New.

To be honest, I am not a great fan of the word 'disruption', because it generates a kind of sympathy that is misplaced. Listening to speakers at a disruption congress, you would think they were trying to save an endangered species: most of the time they talk about how to resist innovation rather than about how to embrace it and adjust to it. Sometimes, they try to motivate companies for change, using cases and examples. However, you get the impression their heart is not always in it. And when the drinks go round at the end of the day, all you can hear is how 'things aren't what they used to be', followed by toasts to 'the good old days'. It has the atmosphere of a lifeboat after the sinking of the 'Titanic': 'We are all in this together and we need to do what we can to survive!' By which they mean as little as possible in terms of change and as much as possible in terms of squeezing the last drops out of their existing business model.

The continuous white line. We are all familiar with this from the highway code. The line you are not supposed to cross. Or from football, where it defines the limits of the playing field. I do not believe in standing still and simply repainting the same white lines. I believe in change and in everything associated with change: trials, tests, renewal, experiments, falling down and getting back up again…

In essence, there are two ways you can respond to the white line when faced with change:

1) Opt for a strategy based on limitations, adding new white lines around your playing field. This means continuing with the old paradigms by

attempting to ignore or laugh away the new, building additional protective walls around your existing business model in the form of new regulations or KPIs that fail to address the real problem.

2) Opt for a strategy based on opportunities and possibilities, removing as many barriers as you possibly can. You need to cross over the white line and see what is beyond it. That is what Elon Musk does. You need to extend the playing field and reinvent the game.

If you experience disruption, you have failed (or did not want) to keep pace with the changes in the world, preferring to remain entrenched in your familiar environment of rules, regulations and patterns. If you take control of the changes in the world, you will be seen by others as a disruptor and will experience no disruption yourself. Disruptors are simply companies that make very clever use of the possibilities that exist. Disruptors are dangerous for others who are not good at reading transformations, cling on to the old rules for too long, and have too little courage to reinvent themselves.

You can also define disruptors as follows: they are entrepreneurs (and companies) who are expert at reading the changes in the world and know in which direction the world will turn as a result. They have a sixth sense for interpreting the expectations and needs of customers. They understand customer desires and frustrations, and use these as the basis for developing their business model. Last but not least, they make smart use of the available technology to serve their customers in the best possible way.

'DISRUPTORS ARE SIMPLY COMPANIES THAT MAKE VERY CLEVER USE OF THE POSSIBILITIES THAT EXIST.'

Live long and prosper

Is the business world under siege? You bet. Who is at risk? Everyone who persists in an old way of thinking, who fails to sufficiently challenge their existing business model or who thinks they are too big and too good at what they do to possibly be under threat. However, the danger zone also includes everyone who clings on to an existing service that could be performed simpler, easier, faster and error-free by new software, with the added benefit of more personal and more comfortable customer care.

Which business models will be the first to fall? The models where customers feel they are being taken for a ride, effectively paying money for little or nothing in return or where the links in the supply chain have too little demonstrable value.

Some companies will go to the wall. Those who evolve in the right manner will survive. New ones will come into existence. The fabric of the market will be reconfigured. The new will build on the old. That is the way it has always been. That is the way it always will be.

This realization is a bit of a bummer if you are in the old banking industry, the old insurance industry, the old car industry, or the old hotel industry. But it can actually be fun if you are a bank, an insurer, a car manufacturer or a hotel. What a liberating feeling! Everything is going to change. Everything will be completely different. Things will never be the same again.

'In the new world, it is not the big fish which eats the small fish; it is the fast fish which eats the slow fish.' So says Klaus Schwab. Klaus Schwab is founder and executive chairman of the World Economic Forum – so he should know. This means that your strategy should no longer be 'let's wait and see what happens and what others do'. The only useful strategy in a disruptive world is 'let us try and do something ourselves, embracing the new and combining it with the good things from the old'. If this strategy works, technology will make it possible for you to speed up and scale up like never before. Because everything is digital. Because the customer is everywhere. Because online is worldwide. But you need to have the guts to see everything as a mirror image, to turn your old business model upside down, and to press on regardless with your process of reinvention and renewal – no matter how strange and unfamiliar it seems at first.

'IT IS NO LONGER THE BIG FISH WHICH EATS THE SMALL FISH; IT IS THE FAST FISH WHICH EATS THE SLOW FISH.'

'Things that do not stay relevant do not even get the luxury of leaving ruins. They disappear'

FACEBOOK'S LITTLE RED BOOK

2

FROM SOCIETY 1.0 TO 5.0

Everyone is a digital citizen

'iPhone is like having your life in your pocket,' said Steve Jobs when the new wonder-device was introduced in 2007. In fact, he was erring on the side of caution. Just ten years later, we now literally hold our life in our hands.

As individuals, we have become both product and producer. Everyone is online. Everyone has a smartphone. And everyone produces data. Every mouse click is data. Every mouse movement is data. Every order is data. Every payment is data. Every sent text message, video and photo is data. Everyone is becoming more and more data. Online, we are telling the world non-stop who we are, how we feel, what we want. We are continuously creating and publicizing our own digital trail. Based on our digital behaviour, we will receive adverts with a blue background instead of a red one, because that suits our digital profile better.

Who collects this data? The bright young men and women who run the new digital platforms: the Googles, Facebooks, Instagrams, Amazons, Baidus and Tencents of the world. Everything we do online makes them smarter. Because everything we do online is logged, cross-referenced and analysed, so that they can serve us better, faster and more efficiently. It even allows them to predict our behaviour.

Data is the new commercial weapon of our times. The physical product is no longer the most important thing. Nowadays, you sometimes get that free of charge, in return for your data. In other words, your data is your payment. There is no such thing as a free app. In fact, nothing is for free. A free app collects your data and passes it on to those who can exploit it. In China WeChat is a super-app, comparable with Facebook and Twitter, but with the difference that you can run various mini-programmes on it, including making payments. The Chinese do everything with WeChat, to such an extent that people look at you as though you are retarded if you take out a credit card. In September 2017, WeChat had more than 902 million daily active users (and more than 980 million monthly active users), which represents a growth of 17% in just a single year. Each day, 38 billion text messages are sent via WeChat. Six hundred million Chinese use the app to make payments in shops or to transfer money to other contacts. The number of social transactions has also increased by 23% in just a year and the number of offline monthly commercial transactions by 280%.[43] Tencent, the owner of WeChat, is eating up the classic banks and insurers.

The battle for your data is now being fought everywhere. The major platforms are even taking their rivalry into your home, with the development of smart-speakers and AI butlers: Amazon Echo, Google Home and the Apple HomePod. Soon, you will be able to give vocal commands in every room in your house. And be listened to, as well. If you have a smart Samsung television, you know that it has standard watching and listening functions as the default setting. Your TV now watches you more than you watch your TV!

If you give ten likes on Facebook, Facebook knows more about you than a casual friend. If you place 70 likes, Facebook knows more about you than your best friend. Every photo, message or video that you post in the cloud is analysed. Each digital citizen is psychologically profiled non-stop and categorized as a pattern of commercial behaviour. All thanks to algorithms, the collection of data and the creation of meta-data.

Amazon is the antichrist for many retailers and, by extension, almost every company leader. On 14 March 2018, Bloomberg published an article with the title 'How Amazon's bottomless appetite became corporate America's nightmare'. The big bad monster Amazon. The first paragraph reads as follows: '*Amazon makes no sense. It is the most befuddling, illogically sprawling and – to a growing sea of competitors – flat-out terrifying company in the world.*' In this way, columnist Shira Ovide expresses exactly what many traditional business managers are thinking.

'No sense'? The Amazon business model is appealingly simple and well-targeted: Amazon goes in search of red oceans. For a long time, a blue ocean strategy was the quick way to fast growth: new markets, preferably with new products. Amazon does the opposite: it looks for saturated markets, because that is where it can pick up most business. The customers are already present and there are always businesses in any market that make mistakes. When they do, Amazon is ready to pounce.

Let me explain. All companies in a red ocean operate on the basis of classic balanced scorecards, KPIs and the pressure of shareholders. As a result, they focus on the internal optimization of operational excellence at the expense of customer focus. In other words, all the red ocean companies imitate each other in a rat-race to be the most efficient but forget to think about their customers and their relationship with those customers. In contrast, Amazon has a very clear view about those customers and what they want: they want things faster, simpler, cheaper and with the least possible friction. The easier a transaction, the more they like it. End of story. In this way, customer obsession and operational excellence become one.

Red oceans are full of customers, who are often not even aware of their frustrations, until they discover a new interaction that is faster, simpler and cheaper. The retail sector is one such red ocean. Since 1994, Jeff Bezos has made optimal use of software as a motor to offer customers a new experience: e-commerce. The capacity of that motor doubles every 18 months (in keeping with Moore's Law). Amazon does not need to explore new markets or dream up new products. It just makes use of what is already there.

This approach irritates traditional companies for two specific reasons. The first is the seeming volatility and unpredictability of the Amazon path. The second is the continuing belief of investors in the Amazon model. These are the same investors who once forced the classic companies into the straightjacket of old scorecards, but now permit a seemingly unviable model to eat up their business.

But appearances can be deceptive. If you understand what Jeff Bezos is really doing, his strategy is simple and consistent. This immediately explains the belief of investors. Amazon is playing with a new set of rules and tools. Amazon does not focus on 'retail', 'entertainment', 'payments' or any of the other classic business models to earn its money. Instead, Amazon uses those existing business models to conquer the world and the treasure they yield is called 'data'. Amazon is a data machine. As is Google. As is Facebook. As are all the other new digital world players, who are fighting a new kind of world war, with your data and mine as the stake. There are two key battlegrounds in this war: stay as close to the customer as possible and collect as much data as possible.

Amazon does this by systematically increasing the number of domains in which it is active. This provides systematically more data, which gives Amazon even better insights into customer expectations and thinking. What is more, Amazon does this using existing business models, which it effectively regards as a unit of production. As a cost centre. Naturally, this is annoying for the models stuck in the old economy. It even seems unfair. Amazon does not need to earn money from retail, entertainment or banking, so it gobbles up the classic companies in these sectors who are still dependent on profit for their survival. For example, the smartphone launched by Amazon in its fight to obtain the world's data was a flop. On the other hand, Amazon Echo is a success and Alexa now lives in millions of American homes. And it will not be long before she crosses the Atlantic Ocean. Alexa might seem cute, but she is actually a weapon in Amazon's battle against Facebook, Apple and Google for our data. If we talk to Alexa, ask her questions, give her instructions, etc., this means we are not doing all these things via our smartphone, a mobile app or Google Search.

Now comes the billion dollar question. If Amazon does not need to make money while it plunders existing business models and if the purpose of all this plundering is simply to collect data, what is the ultimate *raison d'être* of Amazon? How does it make its profit? Where is the ROI?

It is all about algorithms. Neural networks (artificial intelligence) are created and 'educated' with all that data. Neural networks function like our brains. Fed by big data, they form algorithmic patterns that can be used to act quickly, efficiently and proactively in response to more limited sets of small data. Automatically. Without the intervention of humans. Robotization, if you like. Amazon makes as many customers as it can and wants to approach each of them individually with 'made-to-measure' offers, communicated through the channel and at the moment that is best for them. It is like a mathematical equation: lots of customers = lots of data = supersmart algorithms = better than ever before service. Digitally. The closer you are to the customer, the more impact you have. The more information you have about each individual, the easier it is to develop new – and even more appropriate – interfaces. That being said, it is still surprising that Amazon would like to move into healthcare?

So, there you have it. Amazon is conquering the world by consuming existing business models, treating them as production units to create smart algorithms that will service customers as frictionlessly as possible, so frictionlessly that we hardly realize what is going on. Every single customer interaction provides yet more data that will make the digital cogs in the giant Amazon machine turn ever faster and ever more powerfully.

Sounds a bit creepy? Big Brother is watching you? Perhaps. A bit. But there is a positive side to the data story.

Thanks to the availability of all this personal data, we do indeed, as consumers, all get a much better and more personal service than ever before. Companies can now respond to our needs 'in the moment'. What is more, the new generation of smart devices makes it easier to predict danger, avoid risks and live more safely.

'WHAT IS 'GOOD' AND 'RELEVANT' IS ALWAYS DETERMINED BY THE CONSUMER.'

If data can make our lives more fun, safer and easier, we are less likely to moan about losing part of our privacy. To survive in the modern marketplace, every company must try to collect as much data as it can about its customers' behaviour. You collect this data by building up a relationship with your customers. Each customer, with the legislator serving as watchdog, will only (continue to) give up data as long as companies treat that data 'well' and provide 'relevant' added value in exchange. What is 'good' and 'relevant' is always determined by the consumer.

Imagine that you check into a hotel and all your personal preferences are already known and have been taken care of: the lighting in your room has been adjusted, the mini-bar is full of your favourite drinks and your interactive room screen is loaded with gastronomic addresses, sight-seeing and entertainment suggestions, as well as films you probably want to watch... This kind of hotel is no longer science fiction. Nexxworks is already working with the Dutch hotel chain citizenM, which uses data to provide each individual guest with a personalized lodging experience.

In other words, citizenM has reinvented the hotel industry. Its business model seems to strongly resemble the model of a classic hotel, but is actually the product of the reflected mirror-image world: it is no longer about renting a room to a guest; it is about providing that guest with an experience. For example, hotel guests at citizenM are asked to do a lot themselves. They check themselves in. They check themselves out. Even so, there are still as many people working in a citizenM hotel as in a normal hotel. The difference? They are not there to run the hotel system; they are there to help customers when they need help or want something. The boring and time consuming tasks that irritate us all have been automated. In fact, they have been turned into a fun factor. Checking in and checking out is usually a hassle, but not at citizenM. It is a new way of doing things and it makes you smile. It also makes you inclined to share the story with others. The personnel are not indoctrinated with the importance of occupancy rates and return. Instead, one of the most important citizenM KPIs is the number of positive posts placed by guests on Facebook, Twitter or Instagram. Fifty-one percent currently post something about their stay at a citizenM hotel. One in two. A good score – and a neat KPI! People post things online either when they are satisfied (the wow-factor) or dissatisfied (the ugh-factor). The guests are therefore a distribution channel that ensures new travellers find their way to citizen M. In the meantime, citizenM has also learnt that their model only appeals to a specific kind of travelling audience. For example, the Chinese and the Americans are wholly unimpressed: the citizenM experience is just too different from Chinese and American hotel culture. If a group from either of these countries arrives at a citizenM hotel, the management can predict with near certainty an increase in the number of negative comments on social media. But this negative talk is not necessarily all bad: it strengthens the 'tribal feeling' of the people who do like the citizenM approach. If people from one 'tribe' read negative comments posted by people from another 'tribe', this simply increases the sense of tribal solidarity: 'See, they do not understand, but we do. That is why we belong here.'

The customer places himself centrally

This is something you hear a lot nowadays: you have got to place the customer in the central position. Customer centricity has become the new holy grail of every organization in the world, from the smallest start-up to the biggest multinational corporation. 'You can find this explicitly on our website and in our mission statement.. It is woven into our DNA and is the bottom line of our strategy… It goes without saying that the customer is central – and has been for years in our company… What is more, we are interested in the total customer and have already defined six different personae … Naturally, we have made the switch to digital, providing advanced solutions for both our staff and our customers… And we have also adjusted our culture to place greater emphasis on a flat hierarchy [but not too much emphasis, because that can be a bit scary]…' Yes, there can be no doubt about it: nowadays, customer is king – or queen. The customer comes first. The customer is our best friend.

'Okay,' I think, 'that sounds fine – but it does not match the way I feel. Your company is not my best friend. And your company does not actually treat me as though I am yours.'

All too often, the assertion that 'we put the customer central' is a hollow claim. Many companies define and implement customer centricity purely from the perspective of their own interests. If managers are honest with themselves, they will be forced to admit that we are not all that obsessed with making our customers happy. There is a difference between saying you put the customer central and behaving in a truly customer-friendly manner. Companies think they are being customer-friendly because their KPI figures tell them so. However, these KPIs are measuring the wrong things and are therefore providing a distorted picture of reality.

I often see how companies try to force new concepts into old paradigms. This means that 'putting the customer central' has to match what the company wants for itself. Consequently, companies believe they are putting the customer first when, in fact, they are putting themselves first. They are pulling the wool over their own eyes!

Most often, companies operate on the basis of a product or service offer. The aim is to provide the product or service to the customer as efficiently as possible. In other words, operational efficiency is key; so key that is governs the entire business process. How can we hunt for new customers as efficiently as possible? What is the most efficient way to keep customers locked in? Once they are locked in, what is the most effective method to manage them? What is the most productive way to upsell and cross-sell? Most crucially of all, how can we create most added value... for ourselves?

Too many companies still fail to understand that in reality the customer actually comes in the last place (or, at best, a low place) in their pecking order. The reason? Companies still try to manage and control things using the principles of the old industrial era. Back then, every process and procedure was focused on operational efficiency, product leadership and market leadership. These controlled processes, and the whole structure, culture and management approach that supported them, had absolute priority over the interests of customers and customer experience, notwithstanding the non-stop protestations that 'the customer always comes first'. This means, for example, that the companies who today still operate a sales department have missed an entire paradigm shift – certainly if the marketing team still reports to sales and the sales people are rewarded on the basis of sales figures, and not on the basis of KPIs that monitor the level and effectiveness of customer experience.

I have always been in favour of putting the customer in the central position, but this must mean something more than simply using a different coloured pencil. Your need to make and colour a completely new customer drawing. Customer centricity is more than just a concept. It is about what 'putting the customer central' actually provides for the customer.

I am ever more realizing that most companies – when it comes to their customers – are unable to say much about what they think is the truth. Or what should be the truth. Or what customers should believe is the truth. Not that this really matters anymore. Those days are gone. It is no longer important 'what the company thinks'; what matters now is 'what the customer thinks'. Your customer does not really care if the words 'customer' and 'central' are mentioned somewhere in your mission statement. All he cares about is receiving a personalized service, when

'MOST COMPANIES USE KPIS THAT MEASURE EFFICIENCY AND SAY NOTHING ABOUT CUSTOMER EXPERIENCE.'

and where he wants it. In addition, he expects respect, speed, transparency and ease. Even more, different customers expect different things. Always and everywhere. It is on that basis that customers will judge your company; not on your mission statement.

Today, the customer is the boss, not the CEO, not the CMO, not the most successful R&D inventor or the most brilliant innovation manager. It is us, the consumers, who have taken power into our own hands – and we have no intention of giving it back.

Faced with this topsy-turvy situation, how can companies persuade customers without offending them? How can you build up customer loyalty? Can you develop a process for this? If so, what kind of process? Do segmentation tools and personae still help? These are the questions that are troubling the mind of many modern-day managers.

In reality, the answer to all these questions is relatively simple, but that is what makes it so difficult to achieve in our complex and changing world. What needs to be central is your relationship with your customer. And it is the customer who determines how intimate that relationship becomes. The task of the company is to maintain the relationship, by making the right value propositions in the right place at the right time. To make this possible, companies must be able to identify what can sweeten the relationship or turn it sour. You have a clean sheet of paper in front of you, marked with three columns: Discard – Keep – New.

The mechanisms for establishing this relationship with your customers are not so very different from those people use in their everyday lives to give 'likes', to relate to others, to offer help and support to each other. What are the keys to any relationship? Interactivity. Connectivity. Not B2B or B2C, but from person to person. In short: how can you make the life of your friend as easy and as pleasant as possible?

The familiar one-to-one

It may seem a bit strange when you see it written down like that. Surely (you might reasonably ask) business has always been based on personal relationships. Have they not? That was certainly true back in the old days. Trade was initially a one-to-one transaction. You had something for me and I had something for you. And that is the way it still is in many places. Small-scale and personal. My baker and me. Me and my baker. He automatically

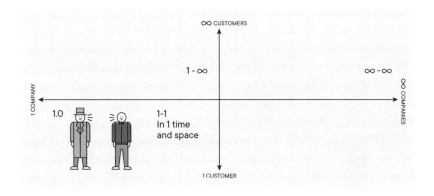

∞ CUSTOMERS

1 - ∞   ∞ - ∞

1 COMPANY

1.0   1-1
             In 1 time
             and space

∞ COMPANIES

1 CUSTOMER

knows the kind of cakes my family loves on a Sunday afternoon. And when I go to collect them, we chat about other things of common interest. The communication between us is like the communication in any good relationship: from person to person. Sometimes one person is the sender and the other the receiver. Sometimes these roles are reversed. As people, we transmit digital data (language) and analogue data (body language). Our conversation partner picks up these signals (through his senses), interprets them using his processing software (patterns of thinking) and other internal information (knowledge, memories, convictions, experiences), before formulating an answer that he then transmits back to us. This is the way good old customer 1.0 interaction used to work. Based on a constant exchange of digital and analogue information, a conversation was developed that allowed a relationship of trust and confidence to be built up.

The disadvantage of 1.0 one-to-one interaction was the limitations imposed by time and space. The conversation partners needed to be in physical contact with each other. Together, at the same time and in the same place. Often a pre-determined place – like a market. On market day, the stallholders came to town and set up the stalls in the market square. And the customer came to the same market square on the same day to see what was on offer. If you were interested in apples and pears, you would enter into negotiation with the fruit seller on a one-to-one basis. The audience of the different stallholders was limited to the people who came to that particular market on that particular day. And once the market was finished, they had to go in search of a different audience on another day in another town. Yet for all these limitations, we can still conclude that the market was the scene of real one-to-one communication.

One-to-∞

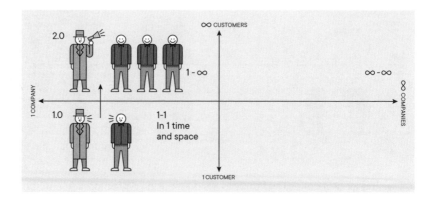

If you only have a select 'club' of customers, it is easy to fit one-to-one discussions with each of them into your agenda. If, however, you work in a large consumer market, it is much more difficult. Fortunately, new means of mass communication eventually offered a number of interesting possibilities to the large-scale 'stallholders' of the late 19th and early 20th centuries. It was now possible to run promotional campaigns on radio and television, to place advertisements in mass circulation newspapers and magazines, to have billboards plastered with 20-metre square posters, or to have cars driven around town festooned with smaller versions of the same.

Mass media technology transformed the marketing world and also the media world. This was the era of the 'influenced customer' and interaction 2.0. The customer relationship was now dictated by one-to-many marketing. The company or the brand dominated all customer communication, which was purely one-way and focused on messages that were no longer aimed at individuals but on consumers as a mass group. In essence, the companies told people what to do. All that was measured in terms of the public's response was the resulting sales figures. It was a system that required little imagination and a lot of advertising.[44]

Thanks to this mass communication model, companies were able to free themselves from the restrictions of time and space in their communication with their customers. They were now at liberty to send messages as often as they liked and were no longer required to interact with customers at a specific place and time. You picked your medium and your message, sent it off and hoped for the best. To give chance a helping hand, you repeated the message regularly, supplementing this with market research and other forms of messaging. The basic premise was that repetition would eventually bring you to your customer's attention. In contrast to the companies, the consumers were still locked in time and space. Individuals had no input in the communication process and no control over when, where and how they would receive the company's message.

In reality, mass communication of this kind is not really communication at all. It is simply a one-directional, one-to-many diktat. There is no question of a conversation, because the customer is never given the opportunity to answer. As a result, there is constant danger of a mismatch. A company books media space and shoots off its message, which lands with a bang in the customer's lap (radio, television, newspaper, etc.). And because every company is doing more of less the same thing, the customer is constantly bombarded with messages. Even so, the companies never know for certain where, when or even if the message was received and, if so, what was the customer's response. You might have spent millions on TV advertising, but it is no use if your customer nips out to make a cup of tea whenever the commercials start. Or if he turns the television off because he has had enough of your badgering.

Of course, it is understandable that every company wants to attract and influence the attention of as many consumers as possible. For this reason, they develop marketing techniques of great ingenuity and sophistication, in the hope that theirs will stand out from the crowd, sometimes stretching the boundaries of what is ethical in the process. We add extra (false) colour and fragrance to make our flowers more appealing than those of our competitors, in the hope that ours will attract the most bees. We send and repeat the same message over and over again, without the slightest intention of eliciting a reply from the receiver. Mass communication has lost all touch with the relational one-to-one communication that typified 1.0 business dealings.

'IF YOU USE MASS COMMUNICATION, YOU HAVE GIVEN UP COMMUNICATING WITH THE CUSTOMER.'

In time, marketers gradually became aware of the limitations of mass communication. You can see this from the way they attempt to extend the sell-by date of the mass communication model through the use of technological add-ons. The first messages still tell you about the basic features and functions of the product, but after that things start getting a bit more technical and psychologically refined. The emphasis switches to '*Freude am Fahren*' and '*Happiness*'. CRM systems make their entrance. So too does segmentation. Personae are developed to better understand consumers as a complex group, expressed in terms of the preferences of an Elizabeth or a John-Paul. Consumer panels and customer feedback gain in popularity and 'the customer journey' becomes the new buzz phrase on everybody's lips.

The technology of CRM systems, personae and the mapping out of customer journeys was intended to get a better grip on customers. There was still an idea that the company was the authoritarian sender and should dominate the relationship. The customer was still someone 'out there', a member of a community of stereotypes. Technology was used specifically for the purpose of repeating the message of what the customer should do in a way that would encourage him to do it more often and more efficiently. The measuring of Net Promoter Score (NPS) was the final refinement of the mass communication model, a last attempt to postpone the model's inevitable decline. You can regard NPS as an after-effect, the last convulsion of a dying system. And if you are still thinking today about introducing CRM, you are living back in the 1990s.

That being said, I have to admit that mass communication worked very well for a long time – at least, if I believe the people who have been familiar with it throughout their career and earned their living (often quite a good one) from it. No-one knows what the customers thought about it, because nobody ever really bothered to measure their response. Even so, many companies today still persist with the one-to-many model, again often because it is what they are familiar with or because the isolation attached to the role of 'sender without receiving' gives them a feeling of control and power. Their KPIs are also geared to this method of communication and these KPIs determine their mindset. It is a Catch-22 situation. Companies are supposedly focused on the customer but still have a predominantly inside-out mentality.

Typically, it is the companies who are most attached to the mass communication model who also use web technology and social media as a mass communication tool, one-to-∞. Sometimes the internet behaviour of the customer may be monitored to get a better understanding of what he wants and provide him with a more focused service. And some companies regularly listen to what consumers are saying online. However, listening-sending and sending-listening are still kept completely separate rather than being simultaneous. The aim is still to control and dominate the relationship with the customer.

Mass communication gives companies a feeling of control. However, all they really control is what they send and how much they pay for it. They cannot control their customers, but because that false feeling of control is so addictive, many companies continue to keep on sending their message, time after time. They achieve a certain customer orientation, but get no closer to their customers than that.

∞-to-one

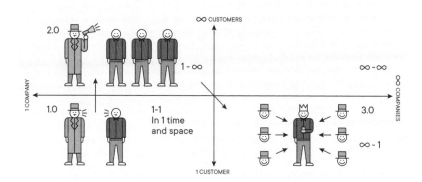

Companies need to realize that one-to-many marketing is a thing of the past. The idea of trying to get a stranglehold on your customers is dead and buried. In recent years, the customer has 'stolen' the power of control from the companies. Technology has changed our behaviour as consumers. And this is not just a generational thing. We have all changed – and changed for good.

The turning point came somewhere between 2009 and 2013. The advent of the smartphone, app culture and the widespread availability of mobile internet shook up the natural order of things like an earthquake. With our smartphone in our hand, we placed ourselves at the centre of our own universe. Every customer became both receiver and sender. Millions and millions of new communication media came into existence. And those media belong to all of us. Today, news is available everywhere and at all times. And that news – good or bad, real or fake – is made by everyone.

Do you remember the debate about comparative advertising? The basic point at issue was this: is it acceptable for the advertising campaign of company A to wipe the

'IT IS NOW THE CONSUMER WHO HAS THE FINAL SAY. AND THE SMARTPHONE IS THE SCEPTRE OF HIS POWER.'

floor with the product of its rival, company B? With us hardly realizing it, this debate has been overtaken by events. Nowadays, everyone and everything is advertising. And if the customer thinks your product deserves to be hammered, he will hammer it. The old paradigm has been turned upside down: it is now the consumer who has the final say. And the smartphone is the sceptre of his power.

This empowered customer has effectively carried out a revolution, and one that the companies are still struggling to come to terms with. The customer has put himself in the central position. Or rather, he has taken this position by storm. As a result, it is no longer possible for companies to say that they will put the customer in the central position. By which I mean: companies no longer have the necessary degree of control to make this possible. The customers have beaten them to it! This also means that many current marketing tools and concepts have lost their value or even become counterproductive. The customer is no longer willing to be bossed around but takes up the position he wants, when he wants, where he wants and how he wants. The modern customer is often better informed than most sales departments and decides for himself what he will listen to and what he will ignore. In the past, the company was the flower, with the customers as bees buzzing around it. Today, the customer is the flower and the companies are doing the buzzing. It is the customer who makes the choices, who decides whether he likes or does not like something, and for how long. There is only loyalty as long as the relationship stays reciprocal.

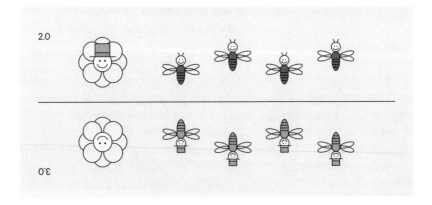

The many-to-one era, in which the empowered customer is now boss, demands a new form of interaction: interaction 3.0. It is no longer just the companies who have been freed from the limitations of time and space (2.0); the customer is now as free as a bird as well. As a result, customer behaviour has changed. Interaction 3.0 was the first step towards turning the world upside down – and it was the mirrored business models that made it possible. On the flip side, the customers who made the switch to these mirrored models also gave them the oxygen that ensured their survival and subsequent success.

'INTERACTION 3.0 WAS THE FIRST STEP TOWARDS TURNING THE WORLD UPSIDE DOWN.'

At the same time, I have also noticed that while customers enjoy accumulating power to themselves, they cannot always handle it. They experience a new kind of stress, because power also brings responsibilities. And when you have the whole world in your hand, it is easy to lose your way amid the multiplicity of available choices and your own ideas about right and wrong.

What will I like? What will I not like? Which opinions count? Which do not? The buzzing of all those bees around your head can drive you mad. Which bees will I give my nectar to? For which bees will I close my paddles? We are living in a world that changes so quickly, with so many options and so little time to process them all, that we constantly feel under pressure. Always online and always multi-tasking, yet still with the feeling we are missing out. Choice stress is our constant companion and occasionally we need to let off steam. As a result, we react more emotionally, more intuitively, perhaps even more superficially. Everything becomes shallow and cursory, and occasionally we post a tweet we later wish we had not posted. More is not always better.

The new customer is still seeking to find his way and sometimes finds it hard to deal with his newly acquired power. At the same time, companies are also engaged in a search of their own. Too many of them have stayed for too long in the one-to-many mode and are now feverishly asking themselves how they can possibly provide as many solutions as there are customers. Consumers might be searching for rest, but so are companies.

'AS CUSTOMERS, WE LOSE OUR WAY AMID THE MULTIPLICITY OF AVAILABLE OPTIONS AND OUR OWN IDEAS ABOUT RIGHT AND WRONG.'

∞-to-∞

Happily for both sides, there is a way out of this uneasy imbalance. You can see its signs everywhere in our hyper-connected world. I am talking, of course, about the groups of consumers who come together on platforms, where they can play an active role. About customers who unite in 'tribes'. About the sharing economy. Consumers interact with each other, place

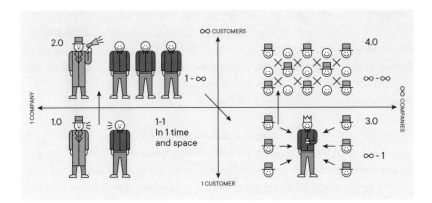

trust in their fellow tribe members, become self-sufficient and design their own products. Consumers want transparency, honesty, speed and short-cuts, and they increasingly rely on peer-to-peer networks of like-minded people to get that. Customers are no longer just customers, but have also become sales, marketing and even infrastructure.

New business platforms attempt to cash in on this evolution. It allows them to eliminate unnecessary intermediaries, while at the same time respond-ing to the unfulfilled needs of the customer. How? By making it easier and more transparent for the customer to make choices. By letting customers share infrastructure. Airbnb does not own a single hotel room. Facebook creates no content of its own. Uber does not have a single taxi. Twitter does not print its own news bulletins. Instead, they facilitate the power and the wishes of the network. '*These companies are indescribably thin layers that sit on top of vast supply systems (where the costs are) and interface with a huge number of people (where the money is)*,' writes Tom Goodwin on tech-crunch.com.[45] This is many-to-many marketing. I also call it customer inter-action 4.0.

The new one-on-one

So, how exactly are companies going to find the rest they so desperately seek? There is only one way: through an upgraded form of one-to-one communication. This means that the companies need to shake them-selves free from their traditional corporate behaviour. In short, they must 'de-brand'. Customers want companies to see them as people. And com-panies must realize that customers can no longer be managed. Unfortu-nately, it can take some time before this latter message finally gets through.

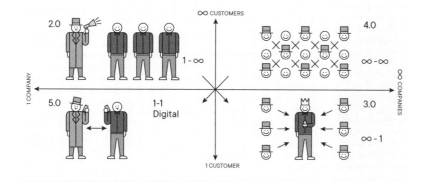

Why? Because many of the company's existing processes are specifically geared to try and exercise this old-style type of control. Even the majority of customer service departments focus on the efficient management of customers, rather than providing them with efficient assistance.

Today, companies must attempt to service each customer individually. The customer wants to be recognized and respected for who he is and wants to experience that he is special. This means that you need to be aware of the customer expectations of all your customers at all times. This is a huge challenge, made more difficult by the fact that different customers have different expectations and even the same customer can have different expectations at different times and in different contexts. The customer wants a personalized value proposition at the moment and within the context that suits him best, communicated by the channel of his choice. And there always needs to be a 'wow'. One hell of a task!

One-to-one	Market	Customer and company both subject to the limitations of time and space	Customer and company are both sender and receiver	Interaction 1.0
One-to-∞	Mass media	Company freed from the limitations of time and space, but the customer still restricted	The sender (company) is in the central position	Interaction 2.0
∞-to-one	Online and mobile technology	Customer and company both freed from the limitations of time and space	The receiver (customer) is in the central position	Interaction 3.0
∞-to-∞	Hyper-connectivity Shared economy Blockchain		Customer and company are both sender and receiver	Interaction 4.0
New one-to-one	The world of everything, mass-individual			Interaction 5.0

The CIA model

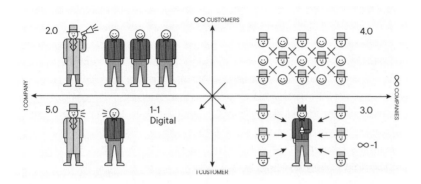

So how do companies actually set about tackling the challenge of new one-to-one (5.0) interaction, while at the same time ensuring the continued efficient management of the other underlying interactions: facilitating the power of the ∞-to-∞ network (4.0); making the customer the centre of his world, in the knowledge that he will no longer allow things to be forced upon him (3.0); serving the customer via mass communication (2.0), where necessary and in keeping with the expectations of the customer within the context of his vision of the new one-to-one relationship (5.0); and, finally, the deployment of real people in the same time and place as the customer (1.0). However complex, this is the only way you can succeed in setting up a direct one-to-one relationship. This is customer interaction 5.0.

c2MxEi

The core task for today's companies is therefore: 'Connect to many and engage individuals'. Emotion and technology must go hand in hand. This can be expressed as a formula:

c2MxEi

A formula of this kind is a useful reminder to keep your house in order. But how do you translate c2MxEi into practice? As a company, how can you connect with numerous customers, yet still engage each one of them as an individual?

'AS PEOPLE, WE ARE CONSTANTLY EXCHANGING DATA, BY WHAT WE SAY, HOW WE LOOK AND HOW WE BEHAVE TOWARDS OTHERS.'

When we talk to others one-to-one – something we do all the time as people – we are constantly exchanging information. Or, if you want to put it another way, exchanging data: by what we say, by how we look, by the way we react to each other, etc. All this data is processed in our heads. If you tell me something, my brain will immediately start to assess whatever information you give, linking it to any other relevant information already stored in its memory, before making any calculations and drawing any conclusions that need to be made, so that I can then give you an answer. If the information you give, received through my senses, triggers my emotions, my answer will be emotionally coloured. Unless, that is, I try to keep those emotions under control, but to do this I will need to make a conscious effort. If your information is emotionally neutral, my answer will have a more rational tint. In other words, before I utter my answer, my brain has already taken several considerations into account and tested a number of variants. And once your brain receives my information, it does exactly the same. The datastream of what I say, how I say it, how I behave and the other signals I send are processed and interpreted by your little grey cells. In this way, we gradually build up a conversation and try to find a connection with each other. We search for words and subjects that can bring us closer together.

As a company, you always want to be present in the moment with your individual customers, even if you have thousands of them. This means that at all times your offer must match the current 'condition' of the customer, a condition that can change with alarming frequency. Connecting with your customer therefore goes much further than saying: 'You have bought A and B, so you might be interested in C'. That is too simple. Your aim must be to provide the customer with precisely the added value that satisfies a particular need he has at that particular moment. You have to offer things without him even asking, which will elicit the response: 'Wow, that is exactly what I need right now!' And of all the available channels of communication, you have to pick the one that you know will most appeal to the customer in the present context. Making all this possible no longer has anything to do with linear thinking. Instead, you need to think in a multi-dimensional space in which even time can be bent. No human being and no spreadsheet, no matter how sophisticated, is capable of doing this.

In a mass market, you can only successfully monitor and process this multitude of different movements by making use of smart digital technology and by analysing and interpreting all current and historical information about the customer, so that you can make the right 'just-in time', 'just-in-place' and 'just-in-content' offer. Machines are capable of continuously collecting details about individual customers, mixing this with context data, processing the result, and then suggesting proactively at exactly the right moment the most appropriate individual answer and the most appropriate gateway through which to communicate it.

I believe in the power of big data, smart algorithms and artificial intelligence.

I also believe it is a huge challenge to find the right balance in the 'man-machine' story.

How and where are you going to use big data, algorithms and AI, and how and where are you going to employ your human talent? For a long time, it was thought that technology would be used to support human staff. In fact, most companies still think, but I am convinced that it will be the task of humans to support the computers, in the few crucial tasks which the computers are still not able to perform.

Intelligent technology will carry out the vast majority of the routine and time-consuming jobs. This will release your human staff to offer customers that little bit extra, that little touch of passion and emotion that can make all the difference. This is an ideal division of labour. Computers are excellent for the type of routine operational tasks where human mistakes can often cause unnecessary customer irritation. However, never make the mistake of trying to 'automate' your people. Let people intervene when their intervention can provide a clear added value. Also allow them more time and freedom to innovate and think creatively. Only automate to eliminate errors and remove negative customer feelings. And also make sure that you never automate existing faults in your system.

What about B2B and the public sector?

This is a question I often hear: 'Your story is all about B2C. So what about business-to business?' This misses the point. The story is not about B2C. It is about people and how they have been changed by technology. Changed in their relationship with the world, with each other and also with companies.

It is equally valid in B2B that the customer must be central and that knowledge of this customer is more important than your products, services and solutions. Likewise, it is equally valid in B2B that the need for a fluent conversation with the other (i.e. the customer company) is a must. And also a challenge. There are often numerous touchpoints between your company and this other company. On both sides. However, in this case the customer is not a person but a circle of people. Maintaining a meaningful conversation with this circle in a B2B context is therefore much harder than with a single customer in B2C. In fact, it is only possible if you digitalize the B2B relationship to the maximum possible extent. Once again, smart algorithms will need to play an increasingly important role. Finally, in B2B it is essential that every customer must be the reason for one of your processes. Customers must never have processes imposed upon them. The customer is the process.

There are four additional reasons why B2B cannot escape the influence of 'the other world'.

Firstly, it is impossible to escape from the wider context. Every B2B is inevitably caught up in the B2C world – and that world has changed dramatically. Your customer might be a company, but the customers of that company are ordinary consumers. If you want to know your customer company through and through, you will need to know how it deals with its own customers. And, above all, with its prospective future customers. Do they have an effective model for the years ahead?

If, for example, you are a leasing company that leases cars to other companies for the use of its personnel, sooner or later your business will be threatened by a variety of developments: increased working from home made possible by digitalization; environmental constraints; the 'mobility as a service' concept, etc. If you know that some companies are already struggling with these issues, there is a perfect red ocean waiting for you, just begging to be explored with your existing customers. Of course, the conversation will need to be different from the past. It should no longer be about cars, but should be designed instead to collect all kinds of other information on the customer. Via all possible touchpoints. In this way, you will discover to what extent each customer is already thinking (or not) about the problems of the future. Perhaps this is nothing new, but in today's rapidly changing world it is more important than ever before.

Secondly, your B2B contacts are also ordinary consumers in their daily lives. They live in the 4.0 world and are an integral part of it. It would be disastrous to interact with them, even in a B2B context, in a 2.0 manner. 2.0 is dead. The standards for 'easy', 'fast' and 'friendly' are now being set by B2C leaders and the bar is being raised all the time. If e-commerce companies can continue to make life easier for their customers, this will soon become the new norm for all companies.

As a result – and thirdly – these digital players are perhaps the biggest threat of all. Where consumers have frustrations and there is a margin to be made, where technology can improve, speed up and simplify interaction with consumers, there will always be digital players to develop an interface between you and your customers, so that they will effectively cut you off from those customers and reduce you to a back-end supplier of products and basic services. They have the means, they have the knowledge and they have the hunger.

Fourthly – and closely related to the previous point – there is the power of the digital network and platforms. Companies will be able to drastically simplify and speed up their processes and workflows, both internally and externally, by replacing the old 2.0 centralist thinking – which is slow, cumbersome and rigid – with the fast, simple, efficient, flexible and much cheaper 4.0 operation of those processes and flows. Blockchain is destined to re-write the entire B2B story, whether companies like it or not.

Once again, the same lesson applies: try to unlearn the bad old ways of the past and learn to think instead in terms of the new reflected world.

This is equally true for the public sector. I have been asked on a number of occasions by organizations in this sector to give talks or organize workshops. These organizations have no customers as such, but nonetheless serve the citizens whose taxes pay their wages. It is only with reluctance that they see any merit in my ideas: 'Do we really need extreme customer centricity if we do not have any customers?'

Replace the C in the CEX of Customer Experience with the C of Citizen and you have the answer to this question. Customer or citizen: their experience of their relationship with companies or government services is just as important. Companies now need to track down customer frustrations and government services must do the same for citizens. Once again, the TREE principle applies: first install the technology, then trawl the red ocean with its frustrations (citizens have no alternative), next secure the engagement of committed citizens and finally unroll the power of the network and the ecosystems. Governments by definition work in a much larger ecosystem than companies.

Government services also need to escape from 2.0 centralized thinking. If they fail to do this, many different kinds of ecosystems will set up their own 4.0 network structures, so that the public sector will risk losing both its function and its functionality. Government and government services were developed in an era when a centralized policy was the only viable option. That is no longer the case...

That being said, companies can also learn a lot from public services and the challenges they face. State authorities have no profit motive. Consequently, the nation's citizens are the only measuring instrument they have to know if they are fulfilling their tasks well or not. The Citizen Experience is their KPI. However, because companies have (and will continue to have) profit as their *raison d'être*, there is a risk that their interest in finding out what people really think will be watered down or pushed quietly into the background. Government authorities do not have that luxury.

'Don't find customers
for your products.
Find products
for your customers.'

SETH GODIN

3

THE HOOKED EMPOWERED CUSTOMER

Connected

 As soon as you write the word 'customer' in capital letters, you have an acronym: CUSTOMER. Each of the letters stands for a typical characteristic of the modern-day consumer. The 'C', for example, stands for 'Connected'. Always connected.

During my presentations, I ask people to swap their smartphone with the person sitting next to them and I set a timer on. At first, there is a little nervous laughter, soon followed by grimaces of unease. There are long seconds of indecision. For many, handing over their 'connecting device' and being without internet is like kicking a drugs habit. It is not easy. We have become *smombies:* smartphone zombies. If you are driving to work and discover you have forgotten your wallet, you keep on driving. If, however, you discover you have forgotten your smartphone, you do an immediate 180 degree turn and speed back home. Nowadays in good hotels, you are given the wifi code before you are even given the key to your room.

Have you got your smartphone with you? There is a good chance you have. What is that you say? The battery is nearly empty? Oh dear! Then you have got a problem. Just think of all the things you are going to miss! If you are one of the people who breaks into a cold sweat at the thought of being deprived of your smartphone, you are suffering from one of the main illnesses of our times: nomophobia or the fear of having no mobile phone. The three greatest anxieties of our generation? No internet, no download, no battery power.

Imagine I had told you five years ago that you would soon be able to do all your banking transactions on your smartphone. You would have thought I was bonkers, but today it is the most normal thing in the world. If you want some idea of the speed with which we all embrace new technology, just open a couple of your drawers at home. I bet they are half full with discarded electronic junk. If you are looking for a business model with a future, you could do worse than think about recycling old telephones and tablets from the urban jungle!

The smartphone, the mobile availability of online mobile and social networks have changed our behaviour. In one way or another, we are all connected. We have become a people of 'swipers' and 'likers', 'frienders' and 'defrienders'. A people that cares more about wifi than about sex. Even more than chocolate. Our way of communicating with each other has changed completely, as has our way of working, the way we divide up our day, our shallowness, our attention span and our focus on things.

On average, we spend two hours a day on social media. However, teenagers always have their media turned on, up to nine hours a day.[46] That is every available moment, except when they are in the classroom or in bed. Connected customers are increasingly using the same tools: two billion monthly active users on Facebook, 500 million on WhatsApp, 284 million on Twitter and 200 million on Instagram.[47] Connected customers are also looking more and more at the same things and using English as their common language. The connected customer thinks universal thoughts, whilst at the same time collecting virtual friends and grooming his virtual personality. And the selfie places us in the centre of our very own virtual shop window. Every 60 seconds we post 510,000 comments on Facebook, 293,000 statuses are updated and 136,000 photos are uploaded.[48]

It sometimes happens that my daughter phones me. My immediate reaction is one of panic. Normally, she never phones. She communicates via texting, on WhatsApp or via Messenger, but never via phone or e-mail. Most young people do not even have an e-mail address anymore. With e-mail you have to wait for an answer. If young people do hold on to an e-mail address, it is only because you often need one for an entry field before you can log in. They prefer apps to software, because access to an app is instant, you do not need to plough through menu after menu and the taste is entirely your own.

Ask a fifteen-year-old what he wants to do later in life and he will often answer something along the lines of: 'Set up a YouTube channel, attract two million followers and make lots of money!' Like, for example, Michelle Phan, a young American entrepreneur who demonstrates make-up on

YouTube and has more than eight million subscribers. Or like PewDiePie, alias Felix Kjellberg, who began on YouTube by replaying various video games and providing a commentary on them in English. Today, he gives uncensored comments on everyone and everything. His channel now has more than 54 million subscribers and has been viewed over 15 billion times. After 'Music', 'Gaming' and 'Sports', it is the best viewed video channel ever on YouTube. Fifteen years ago, Felix Kjellberg would have taken his idea to a television company and would almost certainly have

been shown the door. Now however, there is a 'community' that decides such things. And there is a platform that offers everyone an equal chance. PewDiePie's films only became relevant when he was able to connect the right platform with the right network.

But do not make the mistake of thinking it is only one generation that communicates in this new manner. True, it is the behaviour of young people that differs most from past norms, but all our behaviour has changed to a greater or lesser extent. People of all ages have adjusted and absorbed technology into their lives. Everyone wants wifi and everyone wants to be connected. Even if it is only to keep in touch with their children and grandchildren. Research carried out in the United Kingdom has shown that the communication of the average adult is conducted for almost 50% through photo messages, messaging and social networks.

Urban

The U in cUstomer stands for 'Urban'. In future, we will nearly all live in cities. At the moment, 54% of the world's population already lives in urban areas. And that percentage is increasing each year. By 2025, more than 60% of us will be urbanized. In Europe, North and South America the figure will be as high as 80%. Cities are the breeding ground for new forms of society and economic activity; the place where technology, networks and people quite literally flow together.

If you look at the West, you can see that the human fabric in our cities is changing rapidly. The population is getting older, greyer and greener. Family structure is becoming more varied, with more singles, more single parents and more large families. And people now live in accommodations that reflect the size of their family or relationship: smaller units, communal units, multi-family dwellings and intergenerational homes. Physical connectivity in the street is now supplemented by virtual connectivity.

New business models are also developed in this new urban environment, often in response to specific needs created by the pressure and sheer busyness of urban living. Consider, for example, the cars that are causing mobility in our cities to grind to a halt. The car is supposed to provide mobility, not hinder it. But if you have too many of them in the same place at the same time and mobility becomes nearly impossible. What is more, all those cars take up lots of space – and space is at a premium in urban environments. To make matters even worse, those cars are only actually in use for a fraction of their life span. Most of the time they are just parked somewhere, gobbling up more space and destroying capital. The answer? The car will gradually be banished from the city. People will learn how to share cars. Streets will become low traffic or traffic free. Not only in residential areas, but also in commercial centres. The entire business model built around private car ownership will soon be replaced by a model that provides access to mobility: mobility as a service.

The cities will also be the driving force behind new modes of entrepreneurship. People will look at various challenges together and combine their efforts to provide collective solutions. Not necessarily physical companies, but virtual peer-to-peer and collaborative sharing platforms, where individuals share possessions and responsibility. If you live close to each other, it is easy to share: a car, a bike, a drill, a lawn mower, energy, a meal, even a home. In this way, people will become both supplier and customer, marketing instrument and infrastructure. This collective economy will also generate a number of spin-off services: we already have Eatwith, Feastly, Deliveroo, Instacart and various others.

At the same time, existing business models can also be reinvented. In the past, all that newspapers provided was news. Today, they help to facilitate the group purchase of gas, electricity and fuel oil for their readers (including the free online ones). In the past, car parks used to stand empty all night. Today, hybrid cars from the surrounding neighbourhood can charge their batteries there. In the past, school classrooms also stood empty all weekend. Today, they are used as a venue for activities organized by the local community. In the past, the roof of a shopping centre was just a roof. Today, it is a solar power station for the generation of energy for society as a whole. And this is just the start.

Self-centred

One word: selfie.
Another word: followers.
And a third word: likes.

Tribal

The new consumer is a mix of apparent contradictions. We place ourselves at the centre of our own little world of opinions, selfies and likes, but at the same time we also seek the comfort and security of being a member of a group, a tribe.

People have always come together to form tribes. Simply because it makes us feel good to be with people who are like us. Punks were a tribe, just like hipsters are a tribe today. Bikers have been a tribe for decades. The only two elements needed to turn a group into a tribe are shared ideas and shared communication. And as far as this latter aspect is concerned, technology has made much more possible in recent years. Tesla has become huge without any form of mass marketing – and its success is based on the power of the network and the tribe who choose to back the brand.

Nowadays, the internet makes it possible to contact every other like-minded person on the planet. If you are interested in car tattooing, you can build up a relationship with car tattooers on the other side of the world. If you are a soft-toy freak, you can share photos of your favourite teddy bear with similar fanatics in China, Australia or even on the South Pole! Battle robots, Harleys from the 1930s, fork-bending... It doesn't really matter. If you can think of it, there is probably already an online community somewhere to celebrate it. Why? Because it is possible and because people want to.

'NOWADAYS, THE INTERNET MAKES IT POSSIBLE TO CONTACT EVERY OTHER LIKE-MINDED PERSON ON THE PLANET.'

Yes, tribes are alive and kicking, more so than ever before. In his book of the same title,[50] Seth Godin explains how the internet in combination with a whole variety of other things that have come to the surface in different societies in recent years has helped to ensure the proliferation of tribes in every corner of the world. *'The internet was supposed to homogenize everyone by connecting us all. Instead what it has allowed is silos of interest,'* says Godin in a TED-talk released to coincide with the publishing of *Tribes:* *'People on the fringes can find each other, connect and go somewhere... And it turns out that it is tribes – not money, not factories – that can change our world, that can change politics, that can align large numbers of people. Not because you force them to do something against their will, but because they wanted to connect.'*[51]

If you read *Tribes*, you will learn that a tribe needs active members. This means in turn that you need to engage people; you cannot convert them. You cannot make them become followers. They must want to belong to the tribe of their own volition. People can also belong to different tribes. Tribes are not a religion. Tribes are participatory, voluntary, self-contained and non-exclusive. And like the ancient tribes of yesteryear, you can recognize their modern variants by their symbols.

The tribes of the 21st century are universal. There is no geography. No time zones. The members of present-day tribes are united purely on the basis of interests and action points. They create their own transnational space and communicate about the same things on the same communication plat-forms (Facebook, YouTube, Instagram, Pinterest). Some of us might not like it, but English is the common tribal language.

'THE WHOLE IDEA OF COMMUNITY THINKING IN ORGANIZATIONS IS A FARCE.'

The universal nature of the tribe means that as a brand you can no longer think in geographical terms. You need to think universally as well. This also means that your competitor no longer lives in the same city or country as you do, but can come from anywhere on the planet. All you need to conquer the world is a business model, a computer, a network connection and inspired guts.

You can regard the success of the Five Star Movement in Italy as the polit-ical rise to power of a tribe. The Five Star Movement was created by the coming together of people who shared a common idea about what should happen in their country. They found each other via social media and their programme was compiled using those same media. The movement has no 'centre' as such. It is really a kind of blockchain political phenomenon. If you ask me to give a modern-day example of a tribe, I would point without hesitation to the Five Star Movement. The question is, of course, whether or not the Five Star tribe can survive its transition into a community – because at some point it is inevitable that its current incoherent structure will need to be organized to fit into the existing political system. It will need to create the centre it currently lacks and distil a single point of the view from the myriad points of view it currently allows. In other words, the Five Star Movement is approaching a turning point. Once it wishes to assume the power it has now gained at the ballot box, it will need to do so within the world order dominated by the existing power cliques. Representatives will have to be appointed and this by definition changes the tribe into a community. In this way, the tribe effectively dissolves itself.

Why a tribe and not a community? I like tribes but I do not like communities – or, at least, I do not like the word 'community'. Whenever you use it, the conversation quickly goes like this: 'Okay, we want a community. Can you build one for us? Now, right away? Good. Let us see if we can find some ambassadors...' The problem is that you cannot actually build a community. Not even if you dangle a tantalizing carrot in front of people's noses. Nor are we evolving, as some people think, towards a society of communities; we are evolving towards a tribal society. Communities are just a little too fake for my liking. In a community, you belong (a bit) because you must (a bit). In contrast, tribes are real. People choose to back them because they want to. And are willing to support them through thick and thin. So if you are a brand, forget it if you think you can build a tribe. You just cannot.

A brand can never 'make' a tribe. However, it is possible that a tribe will grow up around a brand, but the brand has no say in the matter. You are living in cloud cuckoo land if you make 'tribe forming' part of your business strategy. This explains why the whole idea of community thinking in organizations is a farce. It is just another way for companies to try and claw back power from consumers. And it will never work. Tribes always develop spontaneously, without central direction. And they develop the way that people – the consumers – want. Tribe forming in terms of brands is only possible when the customer wants to share and exchange his brand experiences with other like-minded fans.

Since brands cannot make a tribe, companies are basically left with two options. One: behave in ways that will make existing tribes love you (and this is only possible if you love the tribes unconditionally in return). Two: become a platform that enables tribes to communicate. Apple does not create tribes, but is accepted as a symbol within a number of pre-existing tribes. Facebook, Instagram, Pinterest, YouTube, etc. offer a place where people can try to form their own tribe or connect with other tribes that have already been formed.

A final word of warning: there is no guarantee on the life expectancy of a tribe. Tribal behaviour is volatile and capricious. If you make a mistake, your fans will soon move to another tribe. Just ask BlackBerry: once mega-hip in business circles, now just an 'ancient Canadian communication device'.

On demand

The new consumer is always in 'on demand' mode, although this does not always mean the same thing. Above all, the consumer wants things at the moment when he needs them. Sometimes that will be now; sometimes it will be in two weeks. If the ink cartridge in my printer has run out, I need a new one and I need it now; if I have ordered a new piece of design furniture from Italy, I do not mind waiting a month for it to arrive. Sometimes an hour is too slow; sometimes tomorrow is really fast. It all depends.

'SOMETIMES AN HOUR IS TOO SLOW; SOMETIMES TOMORROW IS REALLY FAST.'

Whether your customer demands an instant solution, answer or delivery or whether he is happy to wait until tomorrow or even next week, one thing he always expects is to be treated with respect. And to be given honest information. And full information. The customer wants to monitor how you are keeping your promise. This is an expectation he has learnt from companies like Amazon. If Amazon can do it, so should you!

Mindful(l)

As consumers (of no matter what: products, attention, status, time, etc.), we allow ourselves to be bombarded by impulses. The pressure not to miss anything is huge. We need to be constantly 'in the picture'. However, if you have access to the offers of the entire world, it is easy to lose yourself in the sheer scale of things. More choice means more choice stress. And there are only 24 hours in a day. In these circumstances, the question that inevitably arises sooner or later is whether you are making the best possible use of your time. On the one hand, we go in search of new impulses; on the other hand, they are driving us half crazy.

Faced with this dilemma, what people need is more clarity. They are looking for signposts that can lead them to greater ease and comfort. They want someone to take on the role of curator, someone who will make a selection for them from of all the many things the world has to offer. This curator function gives an opportunity to retailers they would be mad to ignore.

As a retailer, you do not need to copy the Amazon model and offer your customers absolutely everything. Your task is to make the right choices for your customer from that everything. The customer comes to you – and keeps on coming back to you – because he likes your approach and the choices you make. And this is something you can even take to extremes.

If you should ever find yourself in Ginza, the luxury shopping district in Tokyo, take a look at Morioka Shoten, which you can find on the ground floor of the Suzuki Building. Morioka Shoten is a small bookstore, just a few square metres large.[52] An average bookstore in Japan sells an average of three or four books per year to its best customers. These customers buy the rest of their books online. Yoshiyuki Morioka sells an average of 30 books a year to his best customers. His secret? He only stocks a single book title at any one time. Each week there is a different new title, but the store also organizes a special exhibition around that title. And during that week the author and the publisher are present in the shop as often as possible to discuss the book with interested buyers.[53] Yoshiyuki Morioka knows exactly what he is doing. In the best Japanese tradition, he is making choice simple. This is mindful: offering people clarity and breathing space. A curator takes the pain out of choosing.

'PEOPLE NEED SIGNPOSTS TO FIND THEIR WAY THROUGH THE ABUNDANCE OF CHOICE THEY HAVE HELPED TO CREATE.'

Many retailers are also looking for a life-raft in these volatile times. They often say: 'We have to go online. We need to think exponentially.' My response is: 'Okay, but think long and hard about the role you want to play.' What is your customer really looking for? Once you have answered this question, focus on it consciously and consistently, even to the point of exaggeration. Do not try and beat Amazon at their own game, because you never can. Why did Amazon buy the Whole Foods health food chain? Because Whole Foods had a reputation as a good curator. You do not visit Whole Foods because you will find every health food product under the sun, but because you will find a selection of the very best products, all carefully displayed and explained. People need signposts to help them find their way through the abundance of choice they have helped to create.

Ethical

The naked truth. No secrets. No hidden costs. No trickery. Consumers want brands that are able to face themselves in the mirror. They want transparency, authenticity, openness, honesty and trust. Consumers are placing their faith more and more in the opinions of peers and less and less in anything to do with central authority. This central authority has shown time and again that it frequently gets things wrong and more often than not is chasing the game instead of being ahead of it. At the same time, stupid companies who think they can outwit the central authority and manipulate customers sooner or later get caught, which only serves to further increase consumer distrust and calls for greater transparency. When consumers reach the limit of their patience, they go in search of other mechanisms that can provide them with the trust they now expect.

As a result, it seems likely that one of the effects of the advent of the universal hyper-connected consumer will be the development of a community with a strong ethical sense. If universal access to information increases people's level of awareness and if increased awareness leads in turn to greater mutual understanding and solidarity, and if these two elements are further strengthened by the power and scale of the network, in which by definition peer-to-peer control is active, then there is every possibility of the role of centralized authority to be taken over by so-called distributed authority, which will increase the ethical sense of the mass of people as a whole.

In short, if you continue to have misery heaped on your head, there comes a point when you want it to stop. And if the politicians will not do it, you become more and more inclined to do it yourself. When this happens, the mass of people put forward ethical goals based on their own situation and devise solutions that will allow those goals to be reached. The result is a shift from central control to a form of decentralized trust, albeit controlled trust. Everyone monitors everyone else.

The digital ledger Blockchain is a good example of distributed trust. Blockchain, as the name implies, is a series of data blocks, in which data from a previous block is used to encrypt data in a subsequent block. Conse-

The Sustainable Development Goals (SDGs) – since 2017 rebranded as the 17#GlobalGoals[1] – are a collection of 17 global goals set by the United Nations.

quently, each new transaction added to the database is always linked to a prior transaction. The ledger is open and distributed. Each addition is automatically sent to every member of the network, which means that each member can check to see whether earlier transactions and blockchains have been conducted according to the agreed rules. Each member can also process data and make a copy of the entire database. Trust in the blockchain concept is derived from the distributed nature of the data in the individual chains and from the fact that it is impossible to amend past transactions. In the past, it was the role of intermediaries to provide this kind of trust in transactions. In Blockchain, that task has been taken over by the mechanism and the network.[54]

Radical

Today's customer behaviour is radical. Black or white. Customers either love you or hate you. They either accept you or reject you. You are a member of the tribe or you are not. Like or dislike, select or deselect, tick or cross, light on or light out: that is how customers think nowadays.

If the boy next door comes up with a brilliant plan that eats away at your business model, before you know what is happening it will be BOOM! Game over. A little bit faster, a little bit easier, a little bit more personal, a little bit cheaper, a few less worries, and all at the time and place most preferable to the customer: it does not take much

'LIKE OR DISLIKE, SELECT OR DESELECT, TICK OR CROSS, LIGHT ON OR LIGHT OUT: THAT'S HOW CUSTOMERS THINK NOWADAYS.'

to blow your business model sky high. Why? Because modern consumers quite literally have all the shops in the world at their fingertips. A few quick swipes and they can buy anything anywhere. Who needs you? Nobody – unless you are really good to them. But woe betide you if you ever tread on their toes. The whole tribe will soon be up in arms against you and you will be frozen out of your market in double-quick time.

You would be surprised how many companies hit the self-destruct button this way. The United Airlines debacle is perhaps one of the best known examples, now included as standard in almost every marketing course in the world. It is April 9th, 2017 and our plane is standing on the tarmac at Chicago airport. Flight 3411 to Louisville is overbooked and no-one is prepared to give up their seat voluntarily. Not even when the company offers compensation of a thousand dollars. Since there are no willing volunteers, the cabin crew decides to select an unwilling one. They pick on David Doa, a doctor of Chinese origin. But he is not having any of it. And so the crew now calls in the airport police to remove him physically. In the film of the incident made by one of his fellow passengers, you can hear him shouting: 'I am not going!', but all to no avail. He is dragged down the aisle and carried kicking and screaming back to the departure lounge. The film, of course, appeared on YouTube soon after and has since had millions of views.[55] Add to this all the online news reports about such outrageous customer-unfriendly behaviour and you can soon see why United Airlines found themselves faced with the mother of all PR problems! The reaction on social media was merciless and nowadays the markets know exactly what that means. Less than a week later the UA share price had plummeted by four percent. An incident lasting just under a minute had wiped 770 million dollars off their stock market value.[56] Was the fault all United Airlines'? You can argue all you like about who said what and who first insulted who. You can claim that there are procedures for overbooking and that the unlucky passenger is selected at random by computer... none of it makes a blind bit of difference. As a company, you cannot treat a customer like this and expect to go unpunished – no matter what the circumstances.

To be honest, United Airlines should have known better. Back in 2009, they had already lost 180 million dollars the same way, after the 'broken guitar' song of Dave Carroll went viral. The song, in which Carroll hammered the UA customer service team for the shoddy way they treated him and his beloved instrument, has been viewed and listened to more than 17 million times. If you Google 'United broken guitar', you get 1,020,000 hits. Google 'Dave Carroll' and you get 13,900,000 hits. I do not know how many hits your name registers, but 13.9 million is an awful lot.

'What do we got?
Right, let's do the math.
Our surface mission here
was supposed to last 31 sols. For
redundancy, they sent
68 sols worth of food.
That's for 6 people.
So for just me, that's gonna last
300 sols which I figure
I can stretch to 400
if I ration.

So I got to figure out a way to grow three years' worth of food here. On a planet where nothing grows. Luckily I'm a botanist. Mars will come to fear my botany powers.'

MARK WATNEY, THE MARTIAN

4

THINKING YOURSELF INTO THE FUTURE

Reverse thinking

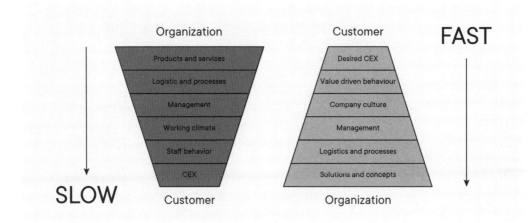

If your relationship with the customer is the most important thing, you must place the customer in the centre of your business model with all the love you can muster.

Every thought, every action and every process must begin with the customer. The key to success is customer experience. Nothing else matters. Processes and solutions are no longer the most important dynamic in your organization: from now on, the customer's wants, needs and emotions are paramount. For many companies, this means a huge transformation. Because all those processes and solutions now need to be redesigned with all those wants, needs and emotions in mind.

If you want to build a relationship with a customer as a friend, the only thing you can measure to determine your level of success is the extent to which you are able to facilitate that relationship. In other words, you measure: 'Is my friend happy with what I offer?' Your entire business model must be built around the needs, desires and expectations of your customer. You must dare to break rules and conventions. You must be prepared to question everything you do. If you have a process, what is its purpose? Is it better for the customer? Is it better for our company? And if it is only better for us, why are we doing it at all?

'IF YOUR RELATIONSHIP WITH THE CUSTOMER IS THE MOST IMPORTANT THING, YOU MUST BUILD UP YOUR ENTIRE BUSINESS MODEL AROUND THE NEEDS OF THAT CUSTOMER.'

Future thinking

The old type of business model – the one that looks from today to the future and assumes that the next ten years will be broadly the same as the past ten years, so that things can carry on in the same old way – has had its day. If you write a plan today for the next ten years, you will never be able to complete it. Not necessarily because it is a bad plan, but because the world changes at a faster pace that your plan foresees. In other words, making a ten-year forward plan is a non-starter. The only thing we can say with any degree of certainty about the year 2030 is that you will no longer be selling the same products and services to the same customers in the same way.

In 1985, the screenwriters for the film *Back to the Future* created their own vision of what things would be like in the decades to come. Using a DeLorean sports car converted into a time machine, Marty McFly travels forwards thirty years to October 21st, 2015. The world of the screenwriters was the world of letters, parcel deliveries, fax machines, telephones and floppy discs. And the film predicted pretty accurately how all these things would change over a thirty year period. All except for modern fax machines. Because there was no internet back in 1985, nor was it even being discussed as a possibility, except in highly specialist circles. Consequently, in *Back to the Future* there is no 'electronic mail', no 'networks' and no 'on demand service'. If Marty McFly had really been able to fly forward thirty years in time, he would have come back with very different instructions for the scenarists!

Looking back, it is now hard to imagine what 1985 was actually like. Many of the things we now see around us in our everyday lives and which form the basis of our economy were no more than possibilities back then. However, it would be wrong to think that everything that has arrived since is brand-new. Apple, Google, Amazon and Uber have all conquered an ocean. Some of them discovered new blue oceans and explored new markets with new products. Others battled their way through red oceans, turning existing markets upside down and colouring the waters an even deeper shade of scarlet.

If we now look forward thirty years, to say 2045, we can be almost certain that there will be new blue oceans to explore. The 'next big things' of 2045 have not yet been developed; in fact, are probably not even on the drawing board yet. However, we can be confident that there will be low-hanging fruit to be plucked. Just as we can be confident that there will be plenty of red oceans, full of discontented customers who are waiting for a parallel offer to appear.

The Martian

Sometimes it is useful to package a message in a story. People like listening to stories. Especially if they contain lots of nice imagery. When we were young, we listened to mum and dad reading out of the big storybook about the dark woods and the big bad wolf. It was a way to warn us as kids about some of the dangers in life. Fairy tales could actually be quite creepy, even nasty. Perhaps that was the idea. Storybooks still exist today but modern kids are more interested in games, YouTube, Netflix or other things 'on demand'. Parents also watch series on Netflix. Or on something else. Nowadays, everyone has their own channel. Watching TV has been freed from the limitations of time and space. But even in these new contexts, fairy stories are still being made. And they still contain a message, a moral and more than a grain of truth. Sometimes these things are hidden under a layer of dust. But they are still there.

The Martian is one of these modern fairy tales. It is the story of astronaut Mark Watney and the Ares III mission to Mars. A sandstorm forces the other members of the mission to return to earth, leaving behind Watney, who they believe to be dead. In fact, Watney has fallen unconscious in the storm and wakes up only to find out he has been abandoned. He is alone and left to fend for himself in a hostile world. Things are looking grim.

Watney needs to survive for four years, until the next planned mission – Ares IV – is scheduled to reach the Red Planet. This forces Watney to think very carefully about his situation. He uses everything he knows and everything in the environment around him to maximize his chances of staying alive. He grows potatoes in an artificial habitat and burns rocket fuel to produce water. He dismantles an old Mars rover and uses the video camera and re-circuited communication panels to contact Earth. He modifies a Mars buggy to make the long journey to the planned landing site of Ares IV. Watney survives by adjusting the building blocks available to him and supplementing them with whatever he has at hand. He develops solutions, starting with the first and most pressing problem, before moving onto the next. In this way, he overcomes difficulty after difficulty. Sometimes it is quite literally a question of 'do or die', but somehow he always manages to pull through. His anarchic

'BUILD FURTHER ON YOUR PROGRESSIVE INSIGHT, LIKE WATNEY ON MARS AND THE BUILDERS OF THE GOTHIC CATHEDRALS IN THE MIDDLE AGES.'

behaviour inspires others. The crew of Ares II break off their return journey to Earth and travel back to Mars, using a slingshot manoeuvre around their home planet. And the American National Aeronautics and Space Administration (NASA) works together with the China National Space Administration to find ways to try and keep Watney supplied.

The Martian has a number of interesting parallels with the business world. Many companies are noticing that strange things are happening in their environment. They can see their objective but find it hard to reach, almost as if they are paralyzed. The Mars fairy tale shows that if you want to survive further than today, you first need to clearly establish what you want to achieve (your goals) and what is stopping you from getting there (the problems). Once you have identified the goals and the problems, set a list of step-by-step priorities. Begin with the most serious problem. First things first. If some of the existing elements available to you are usable, use them, but supplement them with new things and combine them in a new way (architecture). Once you have solved the first problem – and only then – move on to the next one. Keep doing this day after day. Using progressive insight, advance step by step towards your final goal. Keep looking to the future and re-evaluate your position constantly. Collect additional resources and employ them innovatively. Find creative people, who can bring passion to your endeavours.

Splitting up a large problem (reaching an objective) into smaller sub-problems (a number of steps) before dealing with them one by one is exactly what Elon Musk does.

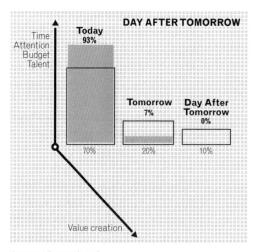

Source: Hinssen (2017)

Strategy for The Day After Tomorrow

If you want to continue creating value, you need to think not only about today, but also about tomorrow and the day after tomorrow. But what strategy must you employ to remain successful? How are you going to allocate your attention, your talent and your budget to get through today, prepare for tomorrow and have something left in reserve for the day after tomorrow? In his book *The Day After Tomorrow*, Peter Hinssen recommends that you should devote 70% of your resources to today, 20% to tomorrow and 10% to the day after tomorrow.[57] To which you will hear most companies reply: 'That is what we're already doing!' However, they are deceiving themselves. Research has shown that in reality they are devoting 93% to today, 7% to tomorrow and nothing at all to the day after tomorrow. If they carry on like this, it is simply the fashions of the day that will determine their future, because they fail to develop any future perspective of their own.

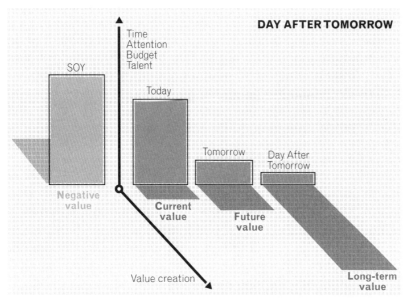

Source: Hinssen (2017)

To make matters worse, many companies are not even dealing with today and tomorrow, but are still too busy trying to clear up the SOY: Shit of Yesterday. I am often under the impression that companies are still stuck in the year 1985: the same business model, the same company structure, the same types of product. Eventually, they wake up and discover that the world around them has changed – but by then it is too late.

It is clear what companies must do. They must turn their focus towards the future. As well as having a business strategy for today and tomorrow, it is vital to allocate sufficient time, budget and talent to the day after tomorrow. You need to imagine the future and visualize how you are going to get there. Using this broad vision of what must be, you need to relate this to what you are doing now and what you plan to do in the immediate years ahead. You must develop actions that pave the way for the vision, actions that connect the future to what you are doing in the here and now.

The value proposition of a company that fails to look forward and the value proposition of a company that thinks several years ahead and translates these thoughts into plans and short-term actions differ significantly over time.

Companies that look ahead tie their value proposition to advances in technology and changes in customer expectations. Such companies are constantly monitoring the technological cloud to identify new innovations that can be useful for what they want to achieve. Where possible, these innovations are integrated into their plans for the future. If, for whatever reason, a technology is not immediately feasible, the necessary steps are taken to make it feasible or find a suitable alternative. The more effectively technology can be absorbed into future plans and the better customer expectations can be identified, the closer the value proposition matches the exponential curve of innovation adoption and the more disruptive the effect of this value proposition will be on companies who have not had the foresight to look to the future.

The value proposition of these latter companies – the ones who fail to think ahead – scarcely improves over time and even in the most beneficial circumstances will probably show at best a modest and steady growth based on incremental innovation (a different colour, different packaging, a slightly cheaper price, etc.). However, if circumstances are not beneficial, the value propositioned might no longer be sufficient to attract customers and the product will go to the wall.

Do you remember the Wartburg cars with two-stroke engines? This is a typical example of a company that failed to look ahead. Ask a young child to draw a car and what you will see is a Wartburg: a square metal box with wheels, with technology to match: if you did not put oil in the petrol tank, the motor seized up! Throughout the entire period that this East German car was built, from 1956 to 1991, almost nothing changed. No new design. No new technical innovations. It was not until 1988 that a 'modern' four-stroke

When the East German world tilted towards the West, it was over and out for Wartburg. Today, the cars only survive in the collections of car freaks and the fantasies of nostalgics.

engine was finally introduced. And for the German Democratic Republic, this was the height of luxury! Who bought a Wartburg? Only the most well-to-do East German citizens. The masses had to make do with the plastic Trabant. But then the Berlin Wall came down and the East German people's image of what a car should be changed forever. Were Wartburg ready to respond to this change in consumer expectations? Of course they were not. That is why today the Wartburg only survives in the collections of car freaks and the fantasies of nostalgics.

The 30/3 rule

The further you look ahead into the future, the freer the space and the bluer the ocean. The more limited your forward vision, the more closely you remain tied to the here and now, the greater the importance of expertise, the stronger the competition and the less room for manoeuvre. The good thing about thinking far ahead is that it gives you as much freedom as your brain will allow. Thinking far ahead is fluid thinking. Only thinking about today is rigid thinking. You really need to be working and planning for the day after tomorrow, tomorrow and today.

How can you do this?

By applying the 30/3 rule.

'WORKING FOR THE DAY AFTER TOMORROW MEANS DARING TO LOOK 30 YEARS INTO THE FUTURE.'

Working for the day after tomorrow means daring to look 30 years into the future. You should already be devoting 10% of your resources to this task.

Based on your assessment of what things will be like in 30 years' time, sketch for yourself a vision of the future. At this stage, this is a broad vision, nothing too detailed. Its purpose is to open people's minds and make them alert to everything that is happening around them. What major shifts do you foresee? How will that affect the future of the company? How can the company remain relevant in this new future? You need to examine the forces that will determine the shape of that future. Technology has set new economic, social, ethical and political cogs in motion. Perhaps within a number of years a new force will come to dominate, connected with a particular shortage or with demography, climate, geopolitics, etc. What needs already exist and which ones are likely to become more critical? Search for the tendencies that seem relevant and valuable for your vision. Once you have found them, continue to take them into account when planning for the future. Forward thinking is the art of de-hyping the hype and giving it the right context and content.

It is not my intention that you should perfectly predict what the world will be like in 2050, so that you can set a dot on the horizon and work towards it. After all, you are not a prophet! It is simply not possible to work out a complete path for the next 30 years. This would require perfect insight into future development, including what new technology will appear and when. You do not have that information. No-one does. So there is no point in fixing a final destination for your 30-year journey. If you do, you are guaranteed to be way off the mark.

'WORKING FOR TOMORROW MEANS TRANSLATING YOUR VISION FOR 30 YEARS AHEAD INTO A PLAN FOR THE NEXT THREE MONTHS.'

Instead, you need to imagine a cloud of possible outcomes, a collection of points towards which it is possible for you to work. Think carefully about the path that will take you step by step in their direction. Thanks to your progressive insight and the knowledge you will acquire during your journey, you will systematically narrow the funnel of possible outcomes. You will gradually learn which points in your cloud are more relevant than others.

In 2012, Ben Barry developed the *Little Red Book* for Facebook. The idea was to outline the key points in the Facebook culture for new members of staff.[58] The book has lots of photos and not much text. Alongside an image of a woman staring at a star-filled sky, you can read: '*With each step forward, the landscape you are walking on changes. So, we have a pretty good idea of where we want to be in six months, and where we want to be in thirty years. And every six months, we take another look at where we want to be in thirty years to plan out the next six months. It is a little bit short-sighted and a little bit not. But any other approach guarantees everything you release is already obsolete.'* Six months. But that was back in 2012. To stay ahead of the game, today, you need to plan for even shorter periods.

'WORKING FOR TODAY MEANS IMPLEMENTING YOUR PLAN FOR THE NEXT THREE MONTHS. YOU SHOULD DEVOTE 70% OF YOUR RESOURCES TO THIS TASK.'

133

THINKING YOURSELF INTO THE FUTURE

Working for tomorrow means translating your vision for 30 years ahead into a plan for the next three months. You should already be devoting 20% of your resources to this task.

This plan should reflect your wider perspectives for the future. Work backwards from the future towards the present, so that you can make the right strategic decisions, the decisions that will allow you to remain sustainably relevant. Every plan for the next three months must contain steps that move you in that direction.

Every company, every business model and every business leader must be obsessively occupied with technology and its impact. Plans relating to technology should never be kept in a rigid form for more than three months ahead. You must have the courage to adjust your technology strategy every three months, if new signals make this necessary.

Working for today means implementing your plan for the next three months. You should devote 70% of your resources to this task.

The balance between fluid and frozen

I will explain how you can best approach the evolution of your company by using Peter Hinssen's theory of the thermo-dynamic cycle of organizations. This theory is described in his book *The Network Always Wins*.[59] As part of this theory, Peter Hinssen introduces the concepts of the super-fluid, fluid, frozen and rigid organization.

A start-up is super-fluid. It can move in any direction, quickly and easily. Starting in the kitchen or outside by the swimming pool: it makes no difference. As the young company grows, some of its processes become fixed and the first layers of structure develop. Contracts are signed that increasingly bind the company to a certain type of behaviour. As a result, the situation evolves from fluid to a little more frozen. A little bit frozen is not a bad thing, says Hinssen. If a particular way of working produces excellent results, it makes sense to keep it. If the core processes can be optimized, this kind of part-frozen mechanism can generate huge profits and prosperity.

Unfortunately, many companies suffer from what might be called deep-freeze sickness. They are characterized by a completely frozen state. If too many things are tied up in their processes or in the hierarchy, so that there is little innovation and little monitoring of the outside world, the company slowly hardens, so that it threatens to become rigid. Why are such companies blind to changes in technology? Because they are sitting in a deep-freeze and have become as hard as rock. And once you become rock, it is hard to become fluid again, unless you throw yourself into the blistering heat of a volcano. Nature teaches us that things that no longer move are dead.

This again shows why it is impossible for a company to continue changing exponentially. To be in a constant state of exponential change, you would also need to be in a constant state of super-fluidity, or at least something very close to it. The moment any of your processes start becoming fixed, even if only slightly, you move from exponential to linear change.

As a company, it is crucial, according to Peter Hinssen, to find the right balance between fluid and frozen. Fluid means that you closely follow what is changing in the world outside your organization and, where necessary, evolve with that change. Frozen means that you opt for business as usual and follow your own linear path.

If you apply this idea of a fluid-frozen balance to companies, it gives you the option to keep some departments more frozen, while allowing others to be more fluid. The different departments are given the fluidity factor that is necessary to successfully realize your plan and book good results.

As a basic rule, the closer a process or department is to the customer (whose expectations have increased exponentially as a result of new technology), the more fluid it should be. The further away from the customer, the more a degree of freezing or even rigidity can be tolerated.

The circle model

Nowadays, a company is not a producer of products but a provider of customer experiences. Consequently, it is vital that your business model is built around the customer. You can think of it as being like the different layers or rings of an onion.

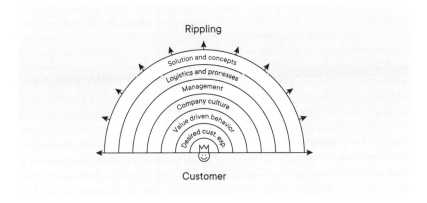

The circle model. An organization is like an onion. The customer is at the core of the organization. The closer things are to this core, the more fluid they need to be.

It is the innermost ring, the core of the onion, which is closest to the heart of the customer. This is the place where you can find all the things that must provide him with the customer experience he desires. The experience you offer must match what he wants as closely as possible at all times. This means that anything that has an impact on customer experience (staff, resources, etc.) must be kept as fluid as possible.

The second ring contains your company's value-driven behaviour. These values allow you to show what your company stands for. They give you your identity. Even so, you need to give your people room for manoeuvre when it comes to the way they translate these values into practice when seeking to satisfy customer needs.

Keep on building your onion outwards, ring by ring, a layer at a time. Think about the way you manage people, about your processes and logistics, and finally about your production.

The circle model looks like what you see when you throw a stone into a pool of water. Where the stone falls, the first waves are abrupt and relatively high.

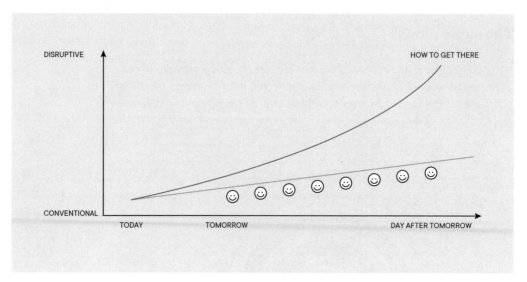

Pirates evolve faster than the organization.

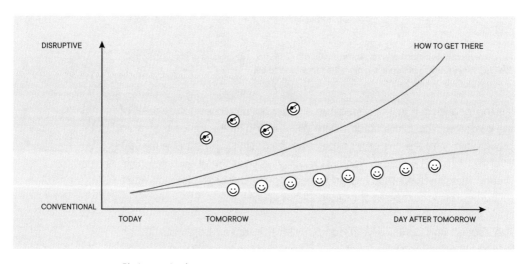

Pirates create piracy.

But as you move away from the point of impact, the ripples become gentler and more gradual. The same goes for your company. In the middle, you need to keep everything moving. The more you work outwards, the more you can move from fluid to frozen. But it is crucial that the rigid level does not become an anchor that weighs down both the organization and its customer experience.

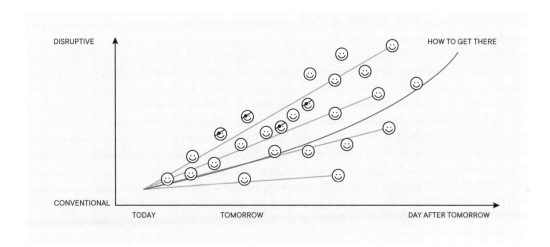

DISRUPTIVE   HOW TO GET THERE

CONVENTIONAL

TODAY   TOMORROW   DAY AFTER TOMORROW

Pirates lift the organization up to a higher level. We can distinguish different speeds within the same organization. For example: extremely fluid 'close to' the customer (as I discussed in the circle model).

So what does this mean in practice? Clearly, you need to keep your one-to-one customer interaction highly fluid, verging on the super-fluid. This means as few fixed processes and hierarchical structures as possible, with a focus on a network structure and plenty of personal job freedom to develop the best possible customer interaction. The production unit at the outer edge of your operations can be kept fairly frozen, bordering on the rigid. It is best to organize your production with clear procedures and plans that allow you to maximize efficiency and effectiveness, because that also works to the benefit of the customer (good price, guaranteed quality, prompt delivery, etc.).

Building different gradations of fluidity into your company across its different departments is a good way to apply exponential thinking, but make sure that your business remains manageable. By regarding your organization not as a monolith but as an amalgam of fluid, less fluid and frozen departments, you will be able to adjust the angle and steepness of your value curve. More fluidity at the right place will result in a steeper incline, which reduces the distance between the experience the customer expects and the experience you offer him.

The pirate model

There is another way you can organize the evolution of your company. You can keep the entirety of your existing organization in a frozen state, whilst at the same time separately testing a variety of radical new ideas. This initially involves maintaining your basic value proposition, which continues to progress in a linear line. The inclination of this line will be dependent on the extent to which you have fluidity in the right places. Running parallel with your classic value proposition, you also experiment with a number of new business models. In concrete terms, this means making people and resources available to identify potential business models, set them up and test them on a trial basis, to subsequently assess whether they can be of use to the company in the future. The message to these 'pirates' is clear: think of something new! If you fail to give these people their head – and just keep plodding on with your current monolithic model – you know that sooner or later you are going to run into trouble.

'MOST COMPANIES FIND IT HARD TO DEAL WITH THEIR PIRATES. BUT ALL YOU REALLY NEED TO DO IS GIVE THEM SPACE.'

I use the word 'pirates' to emphasize the importance of allowing these people to work without fear or restriction. They must be dauntless, like true pirates. They must have the freedom to break all the rules and ignore the company culture, if necessary replacing them with new rules and a new culture. Their task is to explore and conquer. Everything is fluid. How do you choose these people? They are the ones who do not fit in a frozen and rigid world; the ones who make bold suggestions and are not afraid to put their head above the parapet; the ones who stand their ground when challenged by others. Most companies find it hard to deal with their pirates, but all you really need to do is give them space.

So how exactly does a pirate strategy work? First, you free up people and resources from your existing operation and place them in a separate unit. You inspire these people – your pirates – with your vision of what is going to happen in the next 30 years and encourage them to explore new value propositions and business models that can match this vision. To achieve this, you allow them to build on technology that is more sophisticated than would normally be found in your company. These new models and offers must mirror customer expectations as closely as possible and must succeed in meeting those expectations. Once again, this means adopting the best available technology.

By testing alternative business models this way, you create a cloud of possible options for the future, each one a potential strategy for the new world. This way, you also create platforms through time, onto which the company can jump and land safely, when the moment is right.

Right from the very beginning, this implies that your relationship with your current business model is not a permanent one. Every business model has a sell-by date. The longevity of a business model is no longer a valid indicator of its worth.

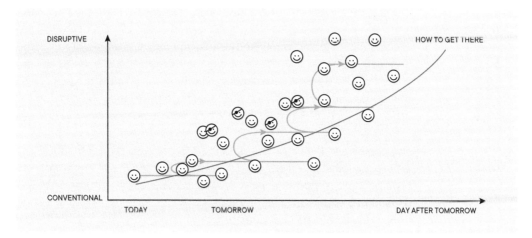

Pirates are always busy building the next platform, to which the rest of the organization can jump when the moment is right, by which time the pirates are already engaged in building the next new model.

Some business models will always be better than others. The same goes for the ideas the pirates test. Some of their experiments will come to nothing, but they must have the freedom to fail – and fail quickly. The winning idea is out there somewhere, but you will only find it by trial and error. And once you have found it, it can be the basis for a new business model, a new company, or perhaps even <u>the</u> new company.

You must let your pirates do their own thing, but you can certainly facilitate their activities centrally. For example, you can provide relevant information about future customer expectations, by having a pool of your people collect and analyse data centrally. You can also centrally define collections of customers for whom it might be useful to think about developing a new value proposition.

Customers do not always say what they expect. As a result, companies sometimes sell themselves short by saying: 'Our customers are not ready for this yet'. Adopting this attitude means that you will always be running behind what the customer really wants. You will never be in the moment with your customer and this can be fatal for your business model. As Henry Ford once said: '*If I had asked people what they wanted, they would have said faster horses.*' Observing customers will teach you much more about their wants and needs than by listening to the stories they tell you. And nowadays, this kind of observation is much easier than in the past. Today, everyone leaves a trail of digital crumbs behind them. With these data crumbs, the pirates strike up a new kind of relationship with the customer.

By carefully mapping wants and needs, you can stay ahead of the game and make customers an offer they cannot refuse. Better still, because your pirates will be the first to make this offer, they will also be in a position to attract the early adopters. And once you have them, they will soon pull in others. That is how things work in today's networked society.

The pirates and their new business models can also have a fruitful effect on the operation of the standard parts of your company. Many companies have become compartmentalized and calcified, not through choice but as a result of their evolution over the years. Pirates have the ability to inspire people in more rigid structures to work more fluidly. And once the new business models take shape and offer more certainty (the prospect of success), more and more people will ask to be a part of them.

'When we came to the valley, no one even wanted to invest in Airbnb. One of the reasons was they thought the idea was crazy. People thought I'd never stay in a stranger's home. That's creepy.'

BRIAN CHESKY, CEO AIRBNB

5

THE NEW
BUSINESS
MODEL

Start with the customer

Start with the customer. Every customer.

Until recently, it was not possible for a company to do so. You had to choose: you could either make the individual customer central (1.0 world) or you could have lots of customers (2.0 world), but be much less close to them. The greater the number of customers, the greater the distance.

Nowadays, things are different. Fundamentally different. Digitalization means that the customer can now demand the central role in the relationship (3.0 world), or demand that you make him feel that way.

As a result, starting with every customer is now possible. And it is something you must do. Without consciously being aware of it, customers have gathered into tribes and united in networks. Within these networks, people pay more attention to each other than to companies. More important still, they are increasingly ignoring the messages of companies. We are developing towards a society without central authority and this clearly has consequences for how customers and companies relate to each other.

This is bad news for the companies that are still stuck in 2.0 thinking. Their traditional approach will work less and less efficiently or even become counter-productive. They can no longer direct or influence their customer base the way they once did. In contrast, every customer is now important and can influence his whole tribe. Companies with a lot of customers stand a long way off from those customers, so that their power will continue to decline as the world tilts further towards the networks.

At the opposite end of the spectrum, the new companies, who think in terms of the new physics, are able to relate to these networks and harness their power as the motor for their success.

Why did I think at the time that Uber and Airbnb were stupid ideas? Because I reasoned from the perspective of the old, centrally directed world. In that world, neither of these models would have worked. They could never have had control over all operations, all interactions, quality, etc. In a network world that is simple: everyone has control. Every user.

In other words, we are talking about distributed authority. Not central control, but shared control. Everyone controls and rewards or punishes everyone else. That is how a blockchain works.

Today, companies can solve the seemingly impossible problem of running their business model by... not running it at all! Instead, they should leave its running to the users. Users who are connected to each other and who consequently can all play a role in its management.

In the past, more customers meant more distance. Not anymore. The more customers a company has, the closer it is able to get to them. The secret that makes this possible is to be found in the 'next big thing', which, like the internet and blockchain, will re-write the way society operates: the combination of big data, artificial intelligence and robotization.

Let us begin with the last of the three. A robot is a non-human 'thing' – a machine, if you like – that takes over human tasks and does them better. Only then are robots useful. That is the economic rationale. Faster, more, better. So far, this replacement function has largely been applied to human actions, but it is now being increasingly applied to human thinking. This brings us to artificial intelligence, a dream that first originated in the 1950s, since when it has died out and been resurrected a number of times, but is now here to stay. Two reasons why. The first is the ever growing power of processors. You need a huge amount of computing power to approach the sophistication of human thinking, but this is now a reality. The second is the fact that companies suddenly discovered an earning model in AI. Artificial intelligence makes it possible to do clever things – more specifically, to 'read' the other (i.e. the customer) – with relatively little data. Like in a human-to-human relationship. Only smarter. Faster. With fewer errors. And able to learn from the few errors it does make. Without preconceptions. Interaction as ones and zeros.

For some years now, we have been teaching 'things' to copy human actions. We programmed what we wanted these things to do and they did it without hesitation. But they were not able to learn. Then we created artificial intelligence. Programmes that after the initial programming can – at least in part – further adjust themselves (within a certain context). In other words, a combination of programming and learning. A bit like how we educate pupils in secondary school. You can think for yourself, but not too much.

After this came the real breakthrough: deep learning. Neural networks. This was no longer programming. More like a smart brain that is comparable with the human mind. These brains are fed on huge quantities of data. And the bigger the quantity, the better. These technological brains learn on the basis of a reward system, just like a human brain. As a baby, your brain is not programmed. It programmes itself in response to all the chaotic influences it picks up from its surroundings. It makes patterns. Algorithms. They allow our brain to calm down, take things a little easier. Once our brain possesses sufficient algorithms to read our environment, we need relatively few impulses to form a picture of something. That is how technological algorithms work as well. They first consume huge amounts of data, so that they can later do lots of things with relatively little new data.

All the new companies like Google, Facebook, Apple, Amazon, Alibaba and Tencent are data-driven. Algorithms are the product of the future. Companies can buy them. Or hire them. And the more they are used, the smarter they become. Just like our human brain. If we use it a lot and keep on feeding it, it gets cleverer and cleverer. Artificial brains are no different. This is a godsend for companies. Their goal as offer providers is to get as close to customers as they can and as fast as they can. This explains why they are all now focusing on three areas: collecting lots of data, investing in artificial intelligence that builds algorithms, and using these to minimize the distance between themselves and their consumers.

The battle for our data has been going on for years. As has the battle to get as close to us as possible. In terms of the western world, things are still pretty even. Google won the battle to be our search engine. Facebook won the battle for our social life and timeline. Apple won the battle to be the device through which we share our data with companies. Amazon also collects astronomical quantities of data about our search and purchasing behaviour, from which it not only earns huge profits but also knits together the segments that penetrate our lives with astonishing speed. However, each of these companies has its challengers. Especially in the Far East, where Baidu, Tencent and Alibaba are even more fiercely at each other's throats in the rat race for data and algorithms.

The battle is focusing more and more on the interfaces between the customer as data producers and the companies as data collectors. Amazon Echo, Google Home and other similar systems are in the process of replacing the smartphone. Apple feels threatened and is looking to develop its own solutions. As is Facebook, which has felt obliged to join the hardware race.

All this effort and the billions of dollars it costs to collect data and build algorithms is designed to achieve that one, all-important thing: to have as many customers as possible, but at the same time to develop a strong relationship with each of them. In fact, to know every customer even better than he knows himself (or herself). To do this, you really do need a superbrain. It all fits together neatly: the more customers you have, the more data you have, the smarter your AI brain becomes and the better you understand your customers. All of them. What once forced companies to make the ultimate choice, now works to exponentially strengthen their position.

This is the new reality: connect to many and engage individuals.

However, your company is probably no Facebook. Or Google. Or Amazon. Or Apple. Or Uber. Or Airbnb. You do not have big data. Should you despair? No. Because you have small data. So, what you need to do from now on is to consistently collect all that data. In comparison, making sales is less important. Small data are crucial, and the more you have, the better. Do not start by trying to think what you are going to do with it. When as a child your brain was learning, you did not decide in advance which data you would absorb and which not. You simply used all the available data to form patterns that were later able to filter the things that were important, less important or not important at all. Companies who try to think in advance what they are going to do with their collected data never learn anything.

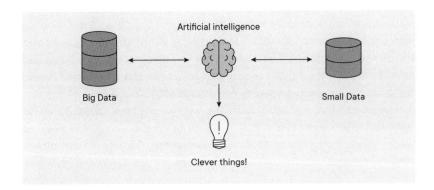

There are two useful things you can do with small data.
1. You can buy or hire algorithms. An algorithm is a brain that has become smart on big data – although not your data. You pay for this brain's knowledge and expertise. Just like you pay an engineer to do smart things. Or a lawyer. Or a marketer. Or an accountant. Or a salesman. You feed the brain with your small data and it finds a way to help you forward. Just like people, but you can't do it without data.
2. Lots of small companies who combine their small data can sometimes do remarkable things together. There are many thousands of small companies all across the world, where the bright young kids of the

future are building neural networks that they feed with small data from tens or even hundreds of thousands of other small companies, who in exchange get access to... a brain. A brain that everyone can use in whatever way they like.

Neural networks show plenty of similarities with... networks. With block-chain. This has nothing to do with programming, but with the power of large numbers in combination with connectivity between all the different participants.

So if, as a manager, you want to get yourself and your company ready for the future, you better make this network world your own. You need to forget about your old familiar 2.0 world and replace it with the unlimited possibilities of the new 4.0 reality.

The customer is no longer a customer. You are no longer the central pivot. A neural network does not have a pivot. Customers strengthen or weaken your business model, as they please. You cannot own customers, like you could in the past. You cannot direct them. Instead, you must learn to listen to them. To understand them. To read them. Every last one.

You can actually use them as part of your company's operations. As sales. As marketing. As quality control. As motivators. As recruiters. As a production unit. Above all, as data producers. It will turn your thinking upside down. Unless you also learn how to think upside down.

Let us start at the beginning. The customer is central. The customer need of every individual customer is central. We now know that we can do this. The more customers we have, the closer we are to them and the better we know them. Thanks to technology. As a company, you want to offer your customer a little bit more than what he needs. To find out more, you collect data. If you look at the companies that have conquered the world, you will see that all they primarily do, is collect data. Only then do they try to sell classic models.

If, as a manager, you want to turn things inside out, so that you can start with the customer, you must first have the guts to create a customer-centred culture. If sales is your most important goal and turnover, margin and profit your only parameters, it is difficult to ask your people to truly put the customer at the centre of everything. However, if your company is focused on learning more about the customer than about yourself; if your company is focused on giving the customer the feeling that he is the centre of everything; and if your company wants to talk like someone with a strong and clear personality, you will need to use other parameters. Sales then become the result of your customer centred approach and a means to collect information about the customer which will further strengthen that approach.

Large companies often ask: 'How can we organize all these changes. How can we manage them? We work with thousands of employees. Worldwide.' My answer is simple. You need to break through the old ways of thinking, internally as well. Move from 2.0 to 4.0. If Airbnb can lease hotel rooms worldwide using the power of the network, it must also be possible for companies with just a few thousand employees to do the same.

The customer shows the way

Attention for the customer must be central in everything you do as a company. The technology you adopt must serve to build up the closest possible relationship with your customers. The more insight you have into changing patterns of human behaviour and the more familiar you are with current and future customer expectations, the easier you will find it to make choices.

Throughout this book, I have repeatedly referred to the need to think ahead, to reallocate your resources, and to turn conventions inside out. Every business model starts by placing the customer at the centre of it. Working for tomorrow means that you explore the needs and desires of customers 30 years ahead and translate that broad vision into a plan for the next three months, which you then implement and adjust day by day. Your progressive insight must show you the way.

It is not new technology that is changing the world. The world is being changed by companies who make that technology their own and understand the paradigm shift it has caused in the thinking and actions of consumers. The large consumer brands who owe everything to the internet also think and act differently in response. What they do represents a new type of economy with new rules, highly technology-driven but also highly focused on human experience. This is how they are able to disrupt the classic business models.

I have spent a lot of time studying large and disruptive business models and the companies who saw everything coming when others saw nothing. And I have eventually come to the realization that their ground plan is actually quite simple. Of course, I do not mean that it is simple to become an Amazon or an Airbnb, but the revolutionary models of this type of company do share a number of common characteristics. I have bundled them together in the following recommendations.

Begin with a daft idea

If someone had dropped the suggested business model of Uber or Airbnb on your desk ten years ago, would you have taken it seriously? And what if someone were to drop a series of equally bizarre suggestions on your desk today? Would you be able to pick out the future winners?

When you are assessing the chances and the possible success rate of a business model, you inevitably – like it or not – make use of the criteria for success and feasibility that you currently have in your head. These criteria have been planted there by years of personal experience, reports about success stories in business journals and your own ideas about what it takes to make the grade in the modern business world. You can support the criteria with theories, figures and opinions you have neatly stored in your memory. This set of theories, figures and opinions forms your paradigm, which, in turn, colours your version of the 'truth'. When you say: 'I cannot see this happening' or 'I do not think that...', this instantly reveals something about the lens through which you view the world and the way you read reality.

If the world and consumer behaviour are being turned upside down, so that the reality of today is being mirrored as the new reality of tomorrow, you are immediately confronted with the need to come to terms with a mirror image of the truth. Perhaps things are possible in this new reflected world that would never have been possible in the old world. Perhaps what was normal in the old world is no longer acceptable in the new. And perhaps – you can probably hear me coming – the criteria, opinions, theories and measuring instruments that were useful in the old world to assess new ideas are no longer applicable in the new topsy-turvy world of today.

The new business models are the old business models, but implemented in a completely different way, with different reasoning, different rules and a different dynamic. As long as your thinking is trapped in the old context, because you do not yet fully understand or accept the rationale of the mirrored digital world, you will find it difficult, if not impossible, to distinguish healthy business models from stupid ones. You cannot assess the chances of future business models unless you fully embrace the new reflected reality. It is perfectly possible that what initially seems like a daft idea might turn out to be a brilliant idea in the upside down world. Perhaps a crazy business model in a saturated market is exactly what is needed to start the next great world company. Will you recognize it when you see it?

If you look at the new inverted digital reality from the perspective of the old world, you will get things horribly wrong. You will not see what you need to see and will make the wrong choices. So, throw away your old rules and measuring instruments. Learn new ones by observing and dissecting. Trust your progressive insight. Ask yourself honestly whether or not you are still trapped in the old paradigm.

It is a good exercise to deconstruct existing disruptive models and analyse in depth exactly how they differ from the old models. Sometimes it is also a good idea to take stupid business ideas seriously – at least until proven otherwise. Test them out. Throw them in the group. The more you hear: 'That is not possible because...', the more interesting the idea potentially becomes. Other good questions are: 'Which customer frustrations does this idea solve?'; 'What kind of customer enthusiasm does the idea stimulate?'; 'In how many markets can the idea work at the same time?'; 'What new customer habits can the idea create?'; ''Which departments will the idea turn upside down?'; 'Which intermediary steps will the idea eliminate?'; 'Who does the idea make superfluous?'; and 'Which hidden resources will be mobilized?'. The more the people in your think-tank nervously start shaking their heads, the greater the likelihood that the idea has serious disruptive potential.

Start in a red ocean

Nowadays, it is the consumer who holds power and offers the market. As a result, it is the companies who have an eye for the needs of these newly empowered consumers and respond to them quickly, that will dominate the markets of tomorrow. If you are one of these innovators, you do not need to find a blue ocean and develop a new audience. All you need to do is create customer enthusiasm in an existing red ocean or offer an alternative that makes customers happier.

The companies that can make the difference and are capable of disrupting the existing order all have a nose for consumer frustrations and changing consumer behaviour. What does the customer want? Faster? More comfortable? More pleasant? Easier? Simpler? More respectful? Empathic? Complete? Sustainable? Free? All of the above?

Once they have tracked down the key customer frustrations, the innovators gear their offer to turn these frustrations into customer enthusiasm. This means that their entire internal organization needs to be 100% dedicated to the concept of placing the customer centrally. To make this possible, they make use of the best available technology.

This means that you must dare to go in search of the kind of customer frustrations that are hidden in any brand-new business model and, once you have found them, be willing to rethink the model from the perspective of the digital, upside down reality. Place the customer and changing consumer behaviour in the central position. For many companies, this means turning their long-term business logic upside down.

Do not develop your new business model in the old world (old rules, old ways of thinking). Develop it instead as a mirror image of that old world, to which you can add new dimensions (new technology options, new role patterns, new product and other chains, virtual processes in place of physical ones, freedom from time and place, etc.).

This point cannot be stressed enough: you cannot develop new business models for the future in the old world; they must be a reflection of this old world in the new. Because the new, reflected business models really do place the customer in a central position, they have a much greater appeal to consumers in general, to such an extent that the old models are systematically eaten away. In this way, one customer after another switches from the old world to the new. Nowadays, internet banking and online shopping have become the new norm. Whoever has been picked up by an Uber driver finds it hard to go back to a 'normal' taxi cab. Whoever has used Dropbox now shakes his head when thinking back to the cumbersome collaborative tools of the past. And how do we keep in daily touch with our family and, increasingly, our business contacts and customers? By telephone? By e-mail? No, in a WhatsApp group.

Do not try to earn money

Start with a daft business idea. Launch it in a saturated market. Reallocate resources and roles. It all sounds very different, does it not? However, not as different as my next suggestion will sound to dyed-in-the-wool managers of the old school: do not try to earn money from your early customers.

When you are building your new upside down reality, it is important not to regard your first group of customers as a cash cow. You should not be aiming to make a quick killing. Your ROI can wait. The focus at the start must be on changing consumer behaviour, and on nothing else. And the way to do this is by offering an excellent customer experience.

It is these first users who persuade their friends to also make the step to the new world. And one by one they do it, creating in the process the most efficient and cheapest sales and marketing machine you could ever imagine. Airbnb, Uber and Instagram never employ expensive marketing campaigns to attract their customers. It is the customers themselves who spontaneously take on the marketing role and share their experiences with their network. It is us, the ordinary consumers, who marshal the forces and unleash the disruption that turns the world upside down.

It is also typical of these disruptive brands that they offer a platform that connects people and creates experiences. In fact, they are not so much a brand as a technology. And that technology is geared (successfully) to encourage interaction and communication. There is no website about the brand. The brand is a platform for sharing experiences. Sometimes these brands do not even need an infrastructure, because this is also provided by the customer and shared on the platform. Airbnb does not own hotels and Uber does not own taxis (or at least not many). Another good example is Instacart, the Uber of food delivery. If you have a bit of spare time, you can become a delivery man for the shopping of people who live near you. Instacart needs no warehouses, no lorries and no drivers, because Instacart has invented something completely new. Its services are made up entirely from things it 'finds'. Instacart matches shopping demand to shopping supply. It works with existing supermarkets and willing shoppers, who use their own cars and smartphones.[60] The lesson from Instacart? You do not always need to break your head to invent or acquire new hardware. It is sometimes enough to connect existing hardware owners/suppliers via software, so that together you can satisfy a customer need to your mutual advantage.

'IT IS US, THE ORDINARY CONSUMERS, WHO MARSHAL THE FORCES AND UNLEASH THE DISRUPTION THAT TURNS THE WORLD UPSIDE DOWN.'

It is facts such as these – that today's customers are involved in the business model to a high degree and even take on a role in sales and marketing; that people are even prepared to 'lend' brands their hard infrastructure – which explains why the new models are so strong at conquering large groups of consumers.

However, perhaps the best example of all is Tesla. On March 31st 2016, the brand launched its Model 3 at an event in Los Angeles, many months before the car was ready to go into production. For a thousand dollars, customers had the option to already reserve a Model 3. They had no opportunity to see the car in a show room or take it for a test drive. There was no fixed date of delivery and even the final end price was far from certain. The company took out no advertising of any kind to promote the car or to clarify the uncertainties. Even so, within hours of the press launch Tesla had received more than 100,000 pre-orders for the Model 3. By April 7th, just a week after the launch, this figure had risen to 325,000.[51] The estimated sales value in just one week's time? Fourteen billion dollars.[52] Entirely without classic marketing. At the time of writing, the expected delivery period for the Model 3 is between 12 and 18 months...

It goes without saying that Tesla thought carefully about its communication, but in its implementation threw all the traditional practices of the car sector out the door. Social media did the rest. In other words, us. The reservation website for the Model 3 is a cross between a crowd-funding platform and the opening of a door to a dream.

If you would be interested to read a more cynical view of the entire mechanism – how customers return time after time to the same product and even provide brands with marketing, sales and hardware – you might like to take a look at the book *Hooked* by Nir Eyal. Investors, he claims, like to work with companies who stimulate the behaviour of customers in a particular direction, so that they can create user habits. And he is right, of course. If a brand succeeds in doing this, it can quickly conquer the world. Moreover, it can do it without the use of any (or only minimal) traditional resources. Conquering the world with zero marketing budget! If you can crack that code, you will be untouchable. The traditional players will be trailing in your wake.

Let people do new things

Gaudí built his first model of his basilica by hanging it upside down from the ceiling, shaping the contours he wanted with weights attached to little pieces of string. For most other outsiders, these contours only became clear when they were reflected in the arches of the finished ceiling. But Gaudi almost certainly had this reflection and clear vision in his mind all the time.

This first rudimentary master plan of the basilica, with its hanging strings, was gradually filled in with more detail. His 'aerial' models set out the broad lines of the design, but photographs and a series of more traditional models in wood and plaster were used to make Gaudi's ideas more accessible for the carpenters and masons who had to build them.

The building logic used by Gaudi was unfamiliar and not immediately apparent to others. Gaudi made use of classic elements – brick and stone, vaults and arches – but he used them in a way they had never been used before. What's more, his plan grew organically. Details were added gradually, during the coffee or between cigarettes. Each day brought new surprises for the assistant architects and building teams. And there is a good chance that the more traditional among them neither liked nor understood what Gaudi was trying to achieve: an unconventional symbiosis between Neo-Gothic and Art Nouveau, in a manner that would today be described as 'organic design'.

Gaudi did not throw out the old, well-known building blocks of the past, but invested them with a new purpose and reality to create a new form of aesthetic. At the same time, he also devised new building blocks and added these to the old ones. It is like he was making a new form of giant LEGO, fitting the pieces together one by one. He reduced the basilica to a series of lines and dots, which he connected in a radically new way. In the process he gave birth to a new paradigm: his own. He surprised friend and foe alike by fundamentally reinterpreting and recycling the identity of what a church should be. Gaudi was a free spirit.

If you want to develop a new building plan for your business, you will need to learn to look at things in a different manner. Stop thinking in terms of limitations. Think instead in terms of possibilities. SWOT analyses and the Porter 5 are *passé*. They limit your thinking. Technology is now advancing so rapidly that what we think is impossible today will become possible tomorrow. And if not tomorrow, soon after or in some other way. So never say that something is 'impossible by definition '. You must believe that everything is 'solvable step by step'. When Elon Musk said he wants to fly people to Mars in less than a decade, everyone thought he was mad. And there are indeed serious obstacles to be overcome. But one by one they are being eliminated.

Learning to look at things differently implies that you need to re-evaluate and give new meaning to all your means of production and all the resources you possess or have access to, prior to re-incorporating them in your new plan in their new, pure form.

In your current – 'old' – business plan, all your resources are allocated a role and a place. For example, customers are given a specific function and position, as are suppliers, distributors, etc. All the different resources relate to each other in a particular way and each element is given a particular weight within the whole. These relationships between the resources ensure that you are able to do the things you need to do to make your business a success. Together, they make up the business chain, the driving force at the heart of your business model. Can you see Gaudí's strings and weights hanging down?

In every business, the means of production – the building blocks of the business plan – relate to each other in this way. They are tied together and locked in position by conventions and patterns of thinking: A will lead to X, B will lead to Y, X and Y together will lead to Z. These conventions and patterns of thinking are the oil that lubricates the wheels of the business model. They hold things together. They determine what is true and what is false, what happens and what does not happen. We agree upon this paradigm with others and, once agreed upon, assume that things will carry on the same way.

The advantage of conventions and patterns of thinking is that they make things clear and efficient. The disadvantage is that they can also have a limiting effect. They can whisper into the ear of company managers that the role of this particular supplier is this and the role of that particular customer is that, and that they always think like this and always want that, as though the relationships in your business model are as fixed and immutable as the stars in the heavens. Or they tell you that something is impossible; that the way things are is the way things will stay; and that anyone who says anything different does not know what he is talking about.

When you are drawing up your new business plan, you should only include the naked resources salvaged from your old plan, stripped of their confusing layer of conventions and patterns of thought. This will provide you with a collection of 'pure' building block or dots that you can join together in a creative manner, in which new agreements and arrangements can be made in accordance with the rules of a new paradigm. It is not easy to free yourself from your past assumptions and ways of thinking or to see your resources as being completely unfettered. It is especially difficult in large organizations, where particular habits have become engrained in the culture over many years. A younger organization will find it easier to join the dots in radical new ways that no-one has previously thought of.

Throw off the shackles of the past. Get rid of everything until only the naked dots – your available resources in their purest form – remain. Use them with freedom and invention to develop a new business model in which you can create new and more meaningful interactions and relationships (hanging new strings, attaching new weights…). This is exactly what start-ups do. They do not necessarily invent something new. In most cases, they simply use and connect existing resources in a different way. They take customer needs as their starting point, think of a new way to satisfy those needs, and then see how they can do it efficiently and effectively, without allowing themselves to be deflected or discouraged by 'old' conventions that try to tell them what is possible and what is not. They make maximum use of the possibilities offered by the digital world to give their business model shape and form. They recycle or up-cycle existing building blocks, developing new technology where necessary, before bringing all these resources together in a unique manner.

By now, it should be clear what you must do. Dissect your current business model until only the naked resources remain. Use these as a core for the reconstruction of a new, upside down reality. Define your ultimate objective and work back from it. Mirror what once was and change the order of things. Make bottom top and top bottom. Ignore established, common sense thinking and rely instead on your own intuitive logic. Re-arrange the resources at your disposal until you have a new architecture that works. Reconnect the dots.

Connect to many, engage individuals

In chapter two of this book I described the evolution towards a new 5.0 one-to-one society. From the old one-to-one world, we first evolved to a one-to-∞ world, then to a ∞-to-one world and a ∞-to-∞ world, before finally arriving back at a new form of one-to-one interaction. An individual contact between the customer and the brand, but digitally supported. This new one-to-one world has a very familiar feel to it, because, like old one-to-one, it once again involves a degree of recognition and intimacy. It is human-to-human. However, the new aspect of this new human-to-human relationship is that it is only made possible by the smart analysis of data. In new one-to-one, data analysis is used to demonstrate the brand's engagement towards the customer on an individual and personal scale.

Companies are often uncertain how best to deal with this new 5.0 interaction. The answer is simple: you must keep all your previous forms of interaction, but in a tuned-up version or at least – to use a newfangled buzzword – enhanced. In other words, 5.0 interaction contains elements of 1.0, 2.0, 3.0 and 4.0. All previously evolved forms of interaction with the customer remain necessary, but with a new filling inside the old outer case.

This means, for example, that today's 4.0 interaction requires you to think how you can make maximum use of your network. How can you use the existing tribes, your customers, to serve as your sales and marketing departments to the maximum possible extent? As far as 3.0 interaction is concerned, you need to ask how you can give every individual customer the feeling that he is the centre of the world, while 2.0 interaction means the companies will still send out messages, but no longer about the product, the service and how big and powerful you are. Instead, customers now expect that your 2.0 communication will reveal your true personality. Yes, your personality as a company or brand.

What do you stand for as a brand? What is your identity? What is your position in the world? What would you go through fire and water for? You do not need to sound like a one-to-one echo of the customer – then you would simply become your customer's slave – but you do need to show a clear and distinct personality. Everyone has a number of favourite brands. As customers, we often choose particular brands (more frequently than we are sometimes aware) because we feel they match who we are as a person (especially if we add an emotional meaning to their consumption). People like to do business with brands and companies where they feel 'at home'. So make sure your corporate personality shines through in your brand, so that the customer (and the tribe) can easily recognize who you are and embrace you.

5.0 and 4.0, 3.0, 2.0 and 1.0 'revisited' all go together. Because you now have so many customers, you will need to use technology to reach them all in the right manner. You will need to collect and analyse data to know exactly when, how and through which channel you can best approach your individual customers. Do not use data to up-sell, deep-sell or cross-sell. Use it instead to make your relationship with the customer warmer and more committed.

'AS PEOPLE, WE ARE
CONSTANTLY MAKING
USE OF MENTAL
ALGORITHMS IN OUR
DEALINGS WITH OTHERS.'

A relationship means taking account of the other person. You can only do that if you know what this other person stands for. What really makes him or her tick? But the opposite is also true. The other person can only take account of your company if you have a clearly defined personality. The use of data to deepen a relationship is something very human.

Building up a person-to-person relationship also involves meeting each other. During these meeting moments, it is important that both sides listen, look, talk, smell... When we are in contact with others, we are constantly sending out and receiving signals. We try to recognize patterns in all this data and on this basis build up a manner of relating to the other person, which we store away in our memory. If I say A, X gets angry. But if I say B and bring C as a present, X will be happy. This is something I have already experienced several times. So if I want to keep X happy in the future, it is better to avoid A and focus on B and C.

Algorithms are also something very human. As people, we are constantly making use of mental algorithms in our dealings with others. By building an algorithm in your head, you do not need to constantly collect and analyse data every time before coming to an insight. An algorithm is therefore a support programme in which a basic insight is translated. This means that when a particular context arises (you meet X), all you need to do is activate the programme. You might have to fill in a number of variables (time, place, experience, etc.), but the basic framework for your interaction with X will be fixed and easily retrieved from your memory.

In this way, the data that companies collect and the algorithms they build are an extended version of human psychology. The more data you can collect, the smarter and more accurate your algorithm will become. However, algorithms must also contain an element of reward. And the reward that companies include in their algorithms are: warmth and engagement.

Data serves to invest the customer relationship with a warmth that will ultimately lead to a connection and mutual engagement. It is exactly the same as when two people meet each other in a one-to-one context. How does a chemistry develop between these two people? Not necessarily because they are like each other, but because they both stand for something clear which they can both respect, a respect they extend to each other's person in the shape of a willingness to look, listen and empathize.

People increasingly look at brands and companies as though they are a person. This means that as a company you need to be a 'good' person: honest, ethical, authentic, responsible and transparent. And what do the first letters of all these qualities spell? Exactly! HEART. And that is what you need if you want to succeed in today's competitive world. You've got to show you have a heart.

Homework

At the end of this book, I would like to set you the following task. Look at your company and your interactions with your customers and complete the checklist you find below. Have you left behind 2.0 thinking? If so, to what extent? If not completely, see this as an objective towards which you can evolve. Apply the insights you have acquired in the preceding pages and, above all, discover how and why everything is interrelated.

1. Are the knowledge and skills of your entire organization primarily focused on understanding you own products, services and solutions or on understanding the customer better than yourself (and perhaps even better than himself)?
2. Do your managers think in terms of limitations and how to get around them or do they think in terms of opportunities and how to seize them?
3. Is your management style based on control (the middle man) or on trust (the network)?
4. Are you trying to find customers for your products or products for your customers?
5. Do you base your action on assumptions or on big data and AI?
6. Are your processes fixed in long-term plans or are they fluid, so that they can constantly be questioned and amended?
7. Do you strive for perfection or is occasional failure accepted?
8. Do you focus strongly on details or do you view things holistically, concentrating on the big picture?
9. Is tomorrow a continuation of today or a first step towards your day after tomorrow?
10. Are your KPIs old style inside-out or new style outside-in measuring instruments?
11. Do you have all different kinds of customer processes or is every customer interaction part of a single process?
12. Do your processes serve to make life easier for your company or for your customers?

13. Is your main priority sending out your own messages or listening to the customer?
14. Is your communication 2.0-broadcasting or do you let your networks work for you?
15. This list is by no means exhaustive. You can add things in or leave things out, depending on the circumstances of your company. It is just my starting suggestion for how you can make good use of this book.

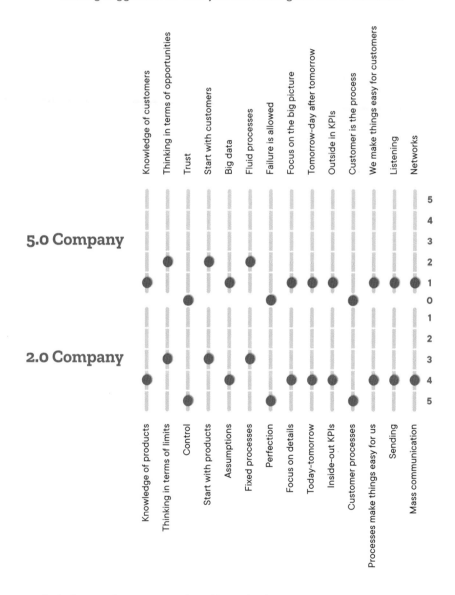

Evolve from a 2.0 to a 5.0 company by working on the above parameters

Three final questions, by way of a parting shot…

1) Does your customer feel like that you know him through and through?[*]
2) Does your company conduct a proper conversation with the customer?[**]
3) Does your customer feel like he is at the centre of everything you do?[***]

The answers to these three questions are your new KPIs.

Even if honesty obliges you to answer 'no' to these three fundamental questions, there is no need to panic. At least you now know in which direction you should be working.

And if you answer three times 'yes', then you are currently on the right track. Just make sure you stay there.

[*] The customer experiences that you know him as soon as your actions take account of the context in which he lives. The more accurately you can read that context and its constituent needs, the more proactively and more surprisingly you can respond to those needs and the greater the customer's feeling of attention.

[**] Most companies still try to lead the conversation. A customer with a question therefore soon finds himself in the company's conversation procedure. The customer talks to department A and two days later is contacted by department B, which asks the same questions. Maintaining a proper conversation with the customer means picking up the thread where you last left off. No matter who contacts the customer, it is important not to create the impression that his time is being wasted. No question should ever be asked twice.

[***] Most customer service centres work with scripts. This means that as a customer your question needs to fit into one of these scripts if you want to be dealt with quickly and correctly. If it does not, then the likelihood of getting a swift answer diminishes. Putting the customer in the centre of everything you do implies that the customer must feel that he or she is the start of the entire process. The aim is to try and automate as much of this process as possible, but in a manner that is as comfortable as possible for the customer. If contact with human personnel is required, this must give the customer the feeling that his or her question is the only thing that counts.

'Sometimes people remember what you say. Sometimes people remember what you do. But they always remember how you make them feel.'

MAYA ANGELOU, POET AND AUTHOR

BIBLIOGRAPHY

Abcouwer, Toon, and Tanja Goense (2013). Balanceren tussen innovatie en traditie. *Informatie* (Lecturer Group (IVI, FNWI) University of Amsterdam) 55-1 (January-February 2013): 36-43.

Antoni Gaudi [Online]. 13 December 2017 [consulted on 14 January 2018], https://nl.wikipedia.org/wiki/Antoni_Gaud%C3%AD

Asano, Evan. *How Much Time Do People Spend on Social Media?* [Online]. 4 January 2017 [consulted on 19 October 2017]; http://www.socialmediatoday.com/marketing/how-much-time-do-people-spend-social-media-infographic

Barra, Marry. *GM 2015 Sustainability Report - To our stakeholders* [Online]. 10 May 2016 [consulted on 10 October 2017]; via https://www.unglobalcompact.org/system/attachments/cop_2017/432711/original/GM_2016_Sustainability_Report.pdf?1509213771

Basilica de la Sagrada Famiglia. *Antoni Gaudi* [Online]. s.d. [consulted on 14 January 2018]; http://www.sagradafamilia.org/en/antoni-Gaudi/

BBC. *BBC Horizon with Arthur C. Clarke (Part 1 of 2)* [Online]. 1964 [consulted on 10 October 2017]; via https://www.youtube.com/watch?v=KT_8-pjuctM.

Beaumont, Claudine. *Bill Gates's dream: A computer in every home* [Online]. 27 June 2008 [consulted on 30 September 2017]; via http://www.telegraph.co.uk/technology/3357701/Bill-Gatess-dream-A-computer-in-every-home.html

Bolt, Martijn. *Wat is blockchain* [Online]. 2012 [consulted on 20 January 2018];via http://watisblockchain.nl/wat_is_blockchain.php.

Bonaire Nieuws nu. *Zeeschildpadden op Te Amo en de problemen waar zij mee geconfronteerd worden* [Online]. 1 August 2016 [consulted on 22 September 2017]; via http://www.bonaire.nu/2016/08/01/zeeschildpadden-op-amo-en-problemen-mee-geconfronteerd-worden/

Brown, Marcel. *IBM Signs A Deal With The Devil.* [Online] s.d. [consulted on 30 September 2017]; via http://thisdayintechhistory.com/11/06/ibm-signs-a-deal-with-the-devil/.

Chang, Emily and Bass, Dina. *Steve Ballmer Says Smartphones Strained His Relationship With Bill Gates* [Online]. 4 November 2016 [consulted on 28 September 2017]; via https://www.bloomberg.com/news/articles/2016-11-04/steve-ballmer-says-smartphones-broke-his-relationship-with-bill-gates

E-estonia. *We have built a digital society and so can you - blockchain* [Online]. s.d. [consulted on 15 January 2018]; via https://e-estonia.com

Office of Ben Barry. *Facebook's Little Red Book* [Online]. s.d. [consulted on 18 October 2017]; via http://benbarry.com/project/facebooks-little-red-book.

Flood, Alison. *Japanese bookshop stocks only one book at a time* [Online]. 23 December 2015. [consulted on 20 October 2017]; via https://www.theguardian.com/books/2015/dec/23/japanese-bookshop-stocks-only-one-book-at-a-time.

Fundaciò Caixa de Pensions (1985). *Antoni Gaudi (1852-1926)*, Editor: Juan Bassegoda Nonell, Translator: A Delannoy, A Leemans, C Sanchez and L Van Waeg. Barcelona: Fundaciò Caixa de Pensions - Algemene Spaar en Lijfrentekas.

Godin, S. (2009a). *Tribes.* Amsterdam: A.W. Bruna Uitgevers.

Godin, S. *Seth Godin over de clans die we leiden* [Online]. February 2009b. [consulted on 6 September 2017]; via https://www.ted.com/talks/seth_godin_on_the_tribes_we_lead/transcript?language-nl

Goodwin, Tom. *The Battle Is For The Customer Interface* [Online]. 3 March 2015 [consulted on 23 August 2017]; via https://techcrunch.com/2015/03/03/in-the-age-of-disintermediation-the-battle-is-all-for-the-customer-interface

Harari, Y.N. (2015). *Sapiens- A Brief History of Humankind.* London: Vintage - Penguin Books.

Harari, Y.N. (2017). *Homo Deus - Een kleine geschiedenis van de toekomst.* Amsterdam: Uitgeverij Thomas Rap.

Harari, Y.N. *Wat verklaart de opkomst van de mens?* [Online]. 24 July 2015 [consulted on 15 November 2017]; via https://www.ted.com/talks/yuval_noah_harari_what_explains_the_rise_of_humans/transcript?language=nl#t-11569

Hinssen, P. (2010). *The New Normal*, Ghent: Mach Media nv, 2010.

Hinssen, P. (2014).*The Network Always Wins.* Sint-Martens-Latem: Mach Media nv.

Hinssen, P. (2017). *The Day After Tomorrow - Hoe overleven in tijden van radicale innovatie.* Leuven: Lannoo Campus & Culumborg: Van Duuren Management

IMEC. *Imec's neuromorphic chip one of '50 Ideas to Change the World'* [Online]. September 2017 [consulted on 2 October 2017]; via https://www.imec-int.com/en/imec-magazine/imec-magazine-october-2017/the-five-highlights-of-september-2017

Instacart. *Press Resources* [Online]. s.d. [consulted on 22 January 2018]; via https://www.instacart.com/press.

Kim, T. *Jamie Dimon says he regrets calling bitcoin a fraud and believes in the technology behind it* [Online]. 9 January 2018 [consulted on 15 January 2018]; via https://www.cnbc.com/2018/01/09/jamie-dimon-says-he-regrets-calling-bitcoin-a-fraud.html

Marinova, P. *Jamie Dimon: Bitcoin Bad, Blockchain Good* [Online]. 13 September 2017 [consulted on 15 January 2018]; via .http://fortune.com/2017/09/13/jamie-dimon-bitcoin-blockchain/

Massachusetts Institute of Technology. *Form-Finding and Structural Optimization: Gaudi Workshop*[Online]. s.d. [consulted on 14 January 2018]; via https://ocw.mit.edu/courses/architecture/4-491-form-finding-and-structural-optimization-Gaudi-workshop-fall-2004/

Morioka Shoten[Online]. s.d. [consulted on 18 October 2017]; https://www.takram.com/projects/a-single-room-with-a-single-book-morioka-shoten/

Piette, F. *Scoop: Porsche mission e, de Tesla-killer!* [Online]. 5 October 2017 [consulted on 6 October 2017];. http://www.vroom.be/nl/nieuws/scoop-porsche-mission-e-de-tesla-killer

Reinsel, D. , Gantz, J. & Rydning, J. *Data Age 2025: The Evolution of Data to Life-Critical Don't Focus on Big Data; Focus on the Data That's Big* [Online]. April 2017 [consulted on 20 October 2017]; via https://www.seagate.com/files/www-content/our-story/trends/files/Seagate-WP-DataAge2025-March-2017.pdf

Reuters Staff. *J.P. Morgan's Dimon regrets calling bitcoin a 'fraud'- Fox* [Online]. 9 January 2018 [consulted on 15 January 2017]; via https://www.reuters.com/article/us-bitcoin-dimon/jpmorgans-dimon-regrets-calling-bitcoin-a-fraud-fox-idUSKBN1EY19W

Rosen, Jonathan. *Flight patterns* [Online]. 22 April 2007. http://www.nytimes.com/2007/04/22/magazine/22birds.t.html?mcubz=0 (consulted on 6 September 2017).

S. L. *The end of Moore's Law* [Online]. 19 April 2015 [consulted on 5 October 2017]; via https://www.economist.com/blogs/economist-explains/2015/04/economist-explains-17

Slezak, M. *Asteroid killed dinosaurs by setting oil alight and spreading soot, says study* [Online]. 14 July 2016 [consulted on 25 September 2017]; via https://www.theguardian.com/science/2016/jul/14/asteroid-killed-dinosaurs-by-setting-oil-alight-and-spreading-soot-says-study.

Steve Jobs - iPhone Introduction in 2007 (Complete) [Online]. 10 January 2013 [consulted on 29 September 2017]; via https://www.youtube.com/watch?v=9hUIxyE2Ns8

ter Voorde, M. *Locatie van meteorietinslag werd dino's fataal* [Online]. 3 April 2013 [consulted on 20 September 2017]; via https://www.nemokennislink.nl/publicaties/locatie-van-meteorietinslag-werd-dino-s-fataal/

The Tesla Team. *The Week that Electric Vehicles Went Mainstream*[Online]. 7 April 2016 [consulted on 12 January 2018]; via https://www.tesla.com/nl_BE/blog/the-week-electric-vehicles-went-mainstream

The Top 20 Valuable Facebook Statistics – Updated September 2017 [Online]. September 2017 [consulted on 12 October 2017]; via https://zephoria.com/top-15-valuable-facebook-statistics/

Toerisme Pastoraal Antwerpen vzw. *De Onze-Lieve-Vrouwekathedraal van Antwerpen, een openbaring. Een bouwgeschiedenis van eeuwen* [Online]. 2018 [G consulted on 14 February 2018]; via https://www.topa.be/nl/antwerp/kerken-in-antwerpen/olv-kathedraal/syllabus/bouwgeschiedenis/

United Nations. *World Cities Report* [Online]. 18 May 2016 [consulted on 30 August 2017]; via http://wcr.unhabitat.org/wp-content/uploads/2017/03/Chapter1-WCR-2016.pdf

Van den Bogaert, R. *De Tesla-killer van Porsche* [Online]. 15 September 2015 [consulted on 19 September 2017]; via http://www.vroom.be/nl/nieuws/porsche-mission-e

Anonymous. *Video shows a passenger forcibly dragged off a United Airlines plane* [Online]. 10 April 2017 [consulted on 30 August 2017]; via https://www.youtube.com/watch?v=VrDWY6C1178

WeChat Lifestyle. *The 2017 WeChat Data Report*[Online]. 9 November 2017 [consulted on 25 January 2018]; via http://blog.wechat.com/2017/11/09/the-2017-wechat-data-report

Wikipedia. *Chicxulubkrater* [Online]. 6 November 2017 [consulted on 17 January 2018]; via https://nl.wikipedia.org/wiki/Chicxulubkrater

Wikipedia. *WeChat* [Online]. 25 January 2018 [consulted on 25 January 2018]; via https://en.wikipedia.org/wiki/WeChat

Wikipedia. *Lohner-Porsche* [Online]. 23 June 2017 [consulted on 15 September 2017]; via https://en.wikipedia.org/wiki/Lohner-Porsche

Wikipedia. *Robert Cailliau* [Online]. 24 July 2017 [consulted on 10 September 2017]; via https://nl.wikipedia.org/wiki/Robert_Cailliau.

Wille, R. *Here's How Much United Airlines Stock Tanked This Week* [Online]. 14 April 2017 [consulted on 10 September 2017]; via http://time.com/money/4739880/united-airlines-fiasco-overbooked-passenger-dragged-stock-price-value/

Wired Brand Lab, and Juniper. *Shyama Rose: Finding success in the never-ending challenge of cybersecurity* [Online]. 2017 [consulted on 22 January 2018]; via https://www.wired.com/brandlab/2017/10/juniper-shyama-rose/?intcid=polar&mvt=i&mvn=7284a9b571bd4277b29a46e2260e68d6&mvp=NA-WIRE-11238836&mvl=Key-ap_native_card+%5BAutopilot+-+Polar+Card%5D

ENDNOTES

1   Toerisme Pastoraal Antwerpen vzw (2018).
2   Toerisme Pastoraal Antwerpen vzw (2018).
3   Fundació Caixa de Pensions (1985).
4   Fundació Caixa de Pensions (1985).
5   Basilica de la Sagrada Famiglia (2018)
6   Antoni Gaudí (2017).
7   Antoni Gaudí (2017).
8   Fundació Caixa de Pensions (1985).
9   Massachusetts Institute of Technology (z.d.).
10 Marinova (2017), Reuters Staff (2018).
11 Kim (2018).
12 Kim (2018).
13 Lohner-Porsche (2017).
14 Wikipedia (2017).
15 ter Voorde (s.d.).
16 Slezak (2016).
17 Bonaire Nieuws nu (2016).
18 Hinssen (2014).
19 Hinssen (2014).
20 Hinssen (2014).
21 Hinssen (2014).
22 Y.N. Harari (2015). *Sapiens. Een kleine geschiedenis van de mensheid.* The Hague: Thomas Rap.
23 Harari (2015, [Online]).
24 Robert Cailliau (2017).
25 E-estonia (s.d.).
26 Marinova (2017).
27 Y.N. Harari (2017). *Homo deus. Een kleine geschiedenis van de toekomst.* The Hague: Thomas Rap.
28 Wired Brand Lab and Juniper (s.d.).
29 Barra (2016).
30 Van den Bogaert (2015), Piette (2017).
31 BBC Horizon (1964).
32 Steve Jobs - iPhone Introduction in 2007 (2013).
33 Chang and Bass (2016).
34 Brown (s.d.), Beaumont (2008)
35 Abcouwer and Goense (2013).
36 Abcouwer and Goense (2013).
37 Abcouwer and Goense (2013).
38 Abcouwer and Goense (2013).
39 S (2015).
40 Reinsel, Gantz and Rydning (2017).
41 IMEC (2017).
42 P. Hinssen (2011).*The New Normal. Explore the limits of the digital world.* Across Technology.
43 WeChat Lifestyle (2017) and Wikipedia (2018).
44 Godin (2009).
45 Goodwin (2015).
46 Asano (2017).
47 Anonymous - The Top 20 Valuable Facebook Statistics (s.d.).
48 Anonymous - The Top 20 valuable Facebook Statistics (s.d.).
49 United Nations (201b).
50 Godin (2009a).
51 Godin (2009a).
52 Morioka Shoten (s.d.).
53 Flood (2015).
54 Bolt (2012).
55 Anonymous, 'Video shows a passenger forcibly dragged off a United Airlines plane' (2017).
56 Wille (2017).
57 Hinssen (2017).
58 Office of Ben Barry (s.d.)
59 Hinssen (2014).
60 Instacart (z.d.).
61 The Tesla Team (2016).
62 The Tesla Team (2016).